J247   Book   6.50
J245CD   Compact Disc   10.00
J245   Book & CD   16.50

RECORDER
Revised Edition

Richard F. Grunow
Eastman School of Music
of the University of Rochester

Edwin E. Gordon
Author, Lecturer
and Researcher

Christopher D. Azzara
Eastman School of Music
of the University of Rochester

STUDENT BOOK TWO

AN INSTRUMENTAL METHOD DESIGNED FOR DEVELOPING AUDIATION SKILLS AND EXECUTIVE SKILLS

INSTRUMENTATION:

SOPRANO RECORDER

FLUTE	TENOR SAXOPHONE	BARITONE B.C.
CLARINET	TRUMPET	TUBA
OBOE	HORN	PERCUSSION
BASSOON	TROMBONE	
ALTO SAXOPHONE	BARITONE T.C.	

VIOLIN	CELLO
VIOLA	BASS

MATERIALS:

TEACHER'S GUIDE FOR RECORDER (J235) • TEACHER'S GUIDE FOR WINDS & PERCUSSION (J90) • TEACHER'S GUIDE FOR STRINGS (J134) • HOME-STUDY CASSETTE (Specify Instrument) •
STUDENT BOOK ONE (Specify Instrument) • HOME-STUDY CASSETTE & STUDENT BOOK ONE COMBINED (Specify Instrument) • ENSEMBLE BOOK ONE (Specify Instrument)
SOLO BOOK ONE—READING (Specify Instrument) • SOLO BOOK TWO—READING (Specify Instrument)
SOLO BOOK THREE—READING (Specify Instrument)
SOLO BOOK ONE—WRITING (J167) • SOLO BOOK TWO—WRITING (J168) • SOLO BOOK THREE—WRITING (J203)
SOLO AND ACCOMPANIMENT COMPACT DISCS AND CASSETTES FOR SOLO BOOK ONE (J99), TWO (J148), AND THREE (J200)
CONCERT SELECTIONS FOR WINDS AND PERCUSSION (Specify Instrument)
SIMPLE GIFTS (Solo Book One for Listening, J202), DON GATO (Solo Book Two for Listening, J201),
YOU ARE MY SUNSHINE (Solo Book Three for Listening, J199)

GIA Publications, Inc., 7404 S. Mason Ave., Chicago, IL 60638

ASSIGNMENT SCHEDULE

The teacher will specify the student's assignments. The student will insert the date and check (✓) underneath the date to indicate specific assignments. The *Home-Study Compact Disc* Track Number is the same as the Item Number.

ROTE SONGS/ROOT MELODIES/ ACCOMPANIMENTS FOR SINGING — Item/Track No.	DATE	DATE	DATE	DATE	DATE	DATE	DATE	DATE	DATE	DATE	DATE	DATE	DATE	DATE	DATE	DATE
1 - Singing "Little Brown Jug" a-Melody b-Bass Line																
2 - Accompaniment for Singing "Little Brown Jug"																
3 - Singing "Simple Gifts" a-Melody b-Bass Line																
4 - Accompaniment for Singing "Simple Gifts"																
5 - Singing "Long, Long Ago" a-Melody b-Bass Line																
6 - Accompaniment for Singing "Long, Long Ago"																
7 - Singing "O Susanna" a-Melody b-Bass Line																
8 - Accompaniment for Singing "O Susanna"																
9 - Singing "A la Nanita Nana" a-Melody b-Bass Line																
10 - Accompaniment for Singing "A la Nanita Nana"																
11 - Singing "Morning Song" a-Melody b-Bass Line																
12 - Accompaniment for Singing "Morning Song"																
13 - Singing "Drunken Sailor" a-Melody b-Bass Line																
14 - Accompaniment for Singing "Drunken Sailor"																
15 - Singing "Old Joe Clark" a-Melody b-Bass Line																
16 - Accompaniment for Singing "Old Joe Clark"																
17 - Singing "Greensleeves" a-Melody b-Bass Line																
18 - Accompaniment for Singing "Greensleeves"																
19 - Singing "...Walkin' Shoes" a-Melody b-Bass Line																
20 - Accompaniment for Singing "...Walkin' Shoes"																
21 - Singing "Winter Day" a-Melody b-Bass Line																
22 - Accompaniment for Singing "Winter Day"																
23 - Singing "Peasant Dance" a-Melody b-Bass Line																
24 - Accompaniment for Singing "Peasant Dance"																
25 - Singing "Yerakina" a-Melody b-Bass Line																
26 - Accompaniment for Singing "Yerakina"																
27 - Singing "Three Young Men from Volos" a-Melody b-Bass Line																
28 - Accompaniment for Singing "Three Young Men from Volos"																
29 - Singing "Monkey Song" a-Melody b-Bass Line																
30 - Accompaniment for Singing "Monkey Song"																
31 - Singing "The Banks..." a-Melody b-Bass Line																
32 - Accompaniment for Singing "The Banks..."																
MELODIC PATTERNS																
33 - "Little Brown Jug" C is DO																
34 - "Simple Gifts" G is DO																
35 - "Long, Long Ago" G is DO																
36 - "O Susannah" F is DO																
37 - "A la Nanita Nana" D is LA																
38 - "Morning Song" D is RE																
39 - "Drunken Sailor" D is RE																
40 - "Old Joe Clark" G is SO																
41 - "Greensleeves" G is RE																
42 - "I'm Gonna Put On My Walkin' Shoes" G is SO																
43 - "Winter Day" G is LA																
44 - "Peasant Dance" D is RE																
45 - "Yerakina" F is DO																
46 - "Three Young Men from Volos" G is LA																
47 - "Monkey Song" B♭ is DO																
48 - "The Banks of Newfoundland" G is DO																

	DATE	DATE	DATE	DATE	DATE	DATE	DATE	DATE	DATE	DATE	DATE	DATE	DATE	DATE	DATE	DATE

TONAL PATTERNS

Item/Track No.

49 - Major - Tonic, Dominant, and Subdominant - Neutral Syllable																
50 - Major - Tonic, Dominant, and Subdominant - Tonal Syllables																
51 - Major - Tonic, Dominant, and Sub. (2.3.4.5) - Neutral Syllable																
52 - Major - Tonic, Dominant, and Sub. (2.3.4.5) - Tonal Syllables																
53 - Minor - Tonic and Dominant - Neutral Syllable																
54 - Minor - Tonic and Dominant - Tonal Syllables																
55 - Minor - Tonic, Dominant, and Subdominant - Neutral Syllable																
56 - Minor - Tonic, Dominant, and Subdominant - Tonal Syllables																
57 - Dorian - Tonic and Subtonic - Neutral Syllable																
58 - Dorian - Tonic and Subtonic - Tonal Syllables																
59 - Mixolydian - Tonic and Subtonic - Neutral Syllable																
60 - Mixolydian - Tonic and Subtonic - Tonal Syllables																
61 - Dorian - Tonic, Subtonic, and Subdominant - Neutral Syllable																
62 - Dorian - Tonic, Subtonic, and Subdominant - Tonal Syllables																
63 - Mixolydian - Tonic, Subtonic, and Subdominant - Neutral Syllable																
64 - Mixolydian - Tonic, Subtonic, and Subdominant - Tonal Syllables																

RHYTHM PATTERNS

65 - Duple - Rests - Neutral Syllable																
66 - Duple - Rests - Rhythm Syllables																
67 - Triple - Rests - Neutral Syllable																
68 - Triple - Rests - Rhythm Syllables																
69 - Duple - Upbeats - Neutral Syllable																
70 - Duple - Upbeats - Rhythm Syllables																
71 - Triple - Upbeats - Neutral Syllable																
72 - Triple - Upbeats - Rhythm Syllables																
73 - Duple - Ties - Neutral Syllable																
74 - Duple - Ties - Rhythm Syllables																
75 - Triple - Ties - Neutral Syllable																
76 - Triple - Ties - Rhythm Syllables																
77 - Unusual Paired - Macro/Microbeats - Neutral Syllable																
78 - Unusual Paired - Macro/Microbeats - Rhythm Syllables																
79 - Unusual Paired - Macro/Microbeats and Divisions - Neut. Syl.																
80 - Unusual Paired - Macro/Microbeats and Divisions - Rhy. Syl.																
81 - Unusual Unpaired - Macro/Microbeats - Neutral Syllable																
82 - Unusual Unpaired - Macro/Microbeats - Rhythm Syllables																
83 - Combined - Macro/Microbeats - Neutral Syllable																
84 - Combined - Macro/Microbeats - Rhythm Syllables																

RECORDER FINGERINGS
Major Tonality - C is DO

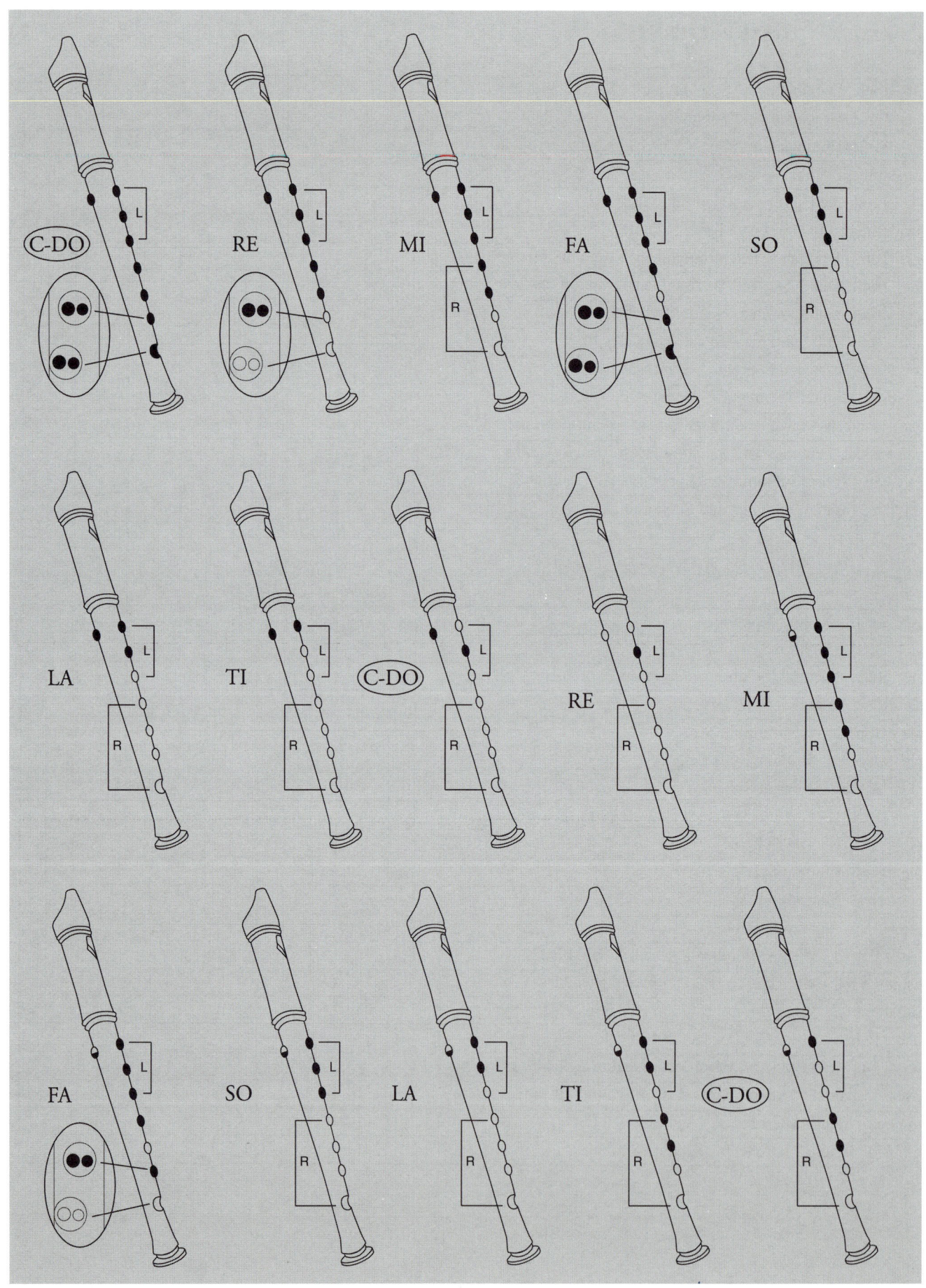

RECORDER FINGERINGS
Minor Tonality - D is LA

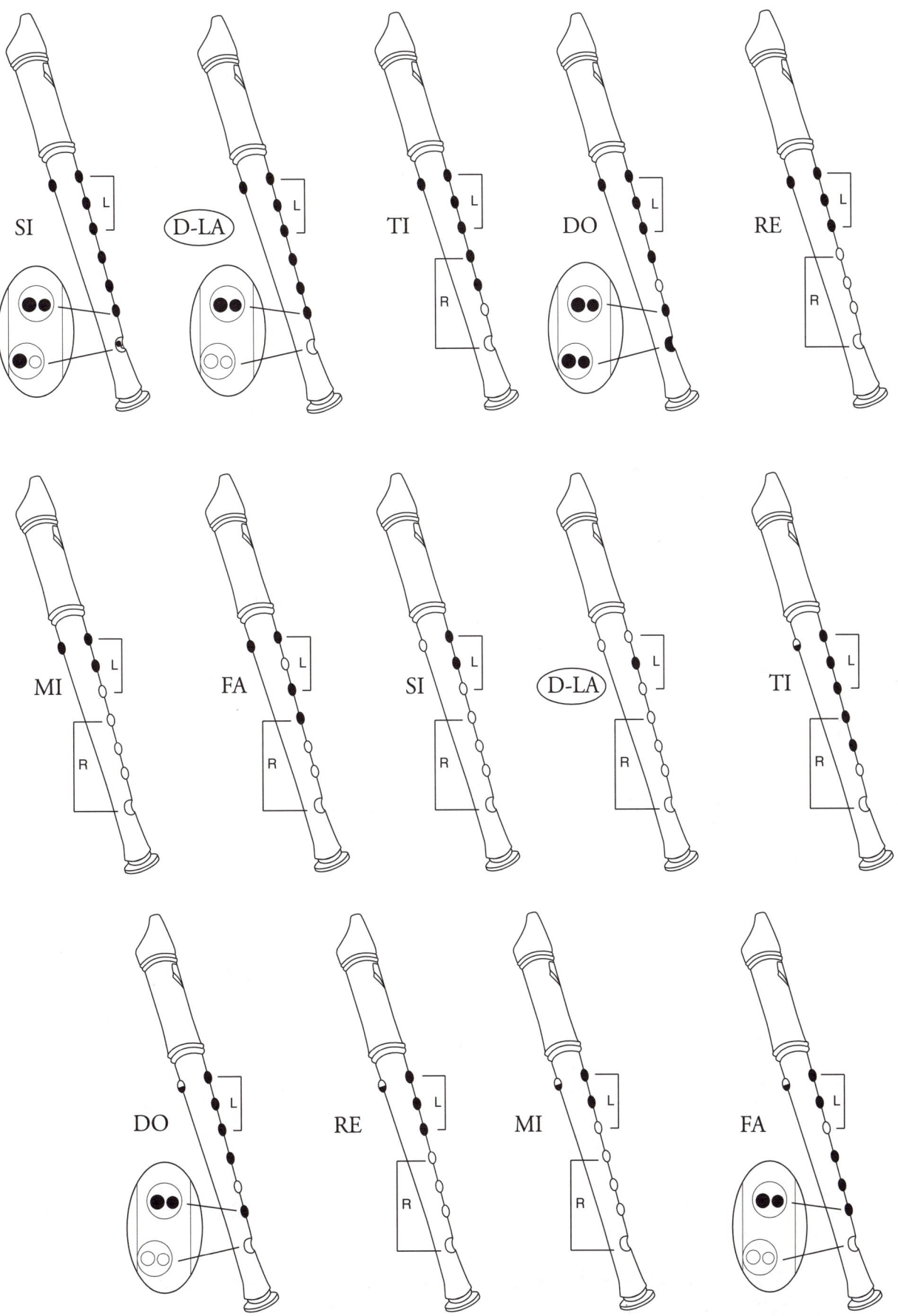

6

TONAL READING
TONIC, DOMINANT, AND SUBDOMINANT FUNCTIONS IN C MAJOR

1. Read the following patterns by singing them WITH TONAL SYLLABLES and by performing them on your instrument. The arrow points to DO. C indicates a TONIC major pattern; F indicates a SUBDOMINANT major pattern; and G7 indicates a DOMINANT major pattern.

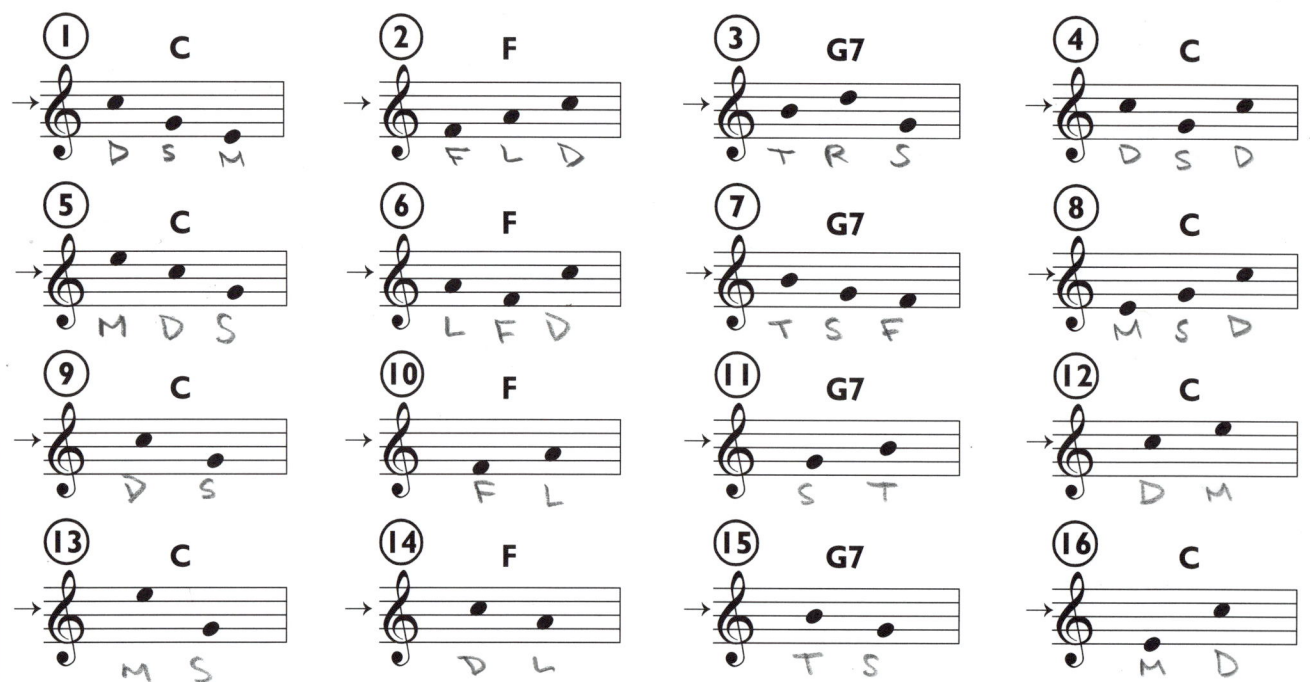

2. Read the following series of patterns by singing them WITH TONAL SYLLABLES and by performing them on your instrument. The arrow points to DO. C indicates a TONIC major pattern; F indicates a SUBDOMINANT major pattern; and G7 indicates a DOMINANT major pattern.

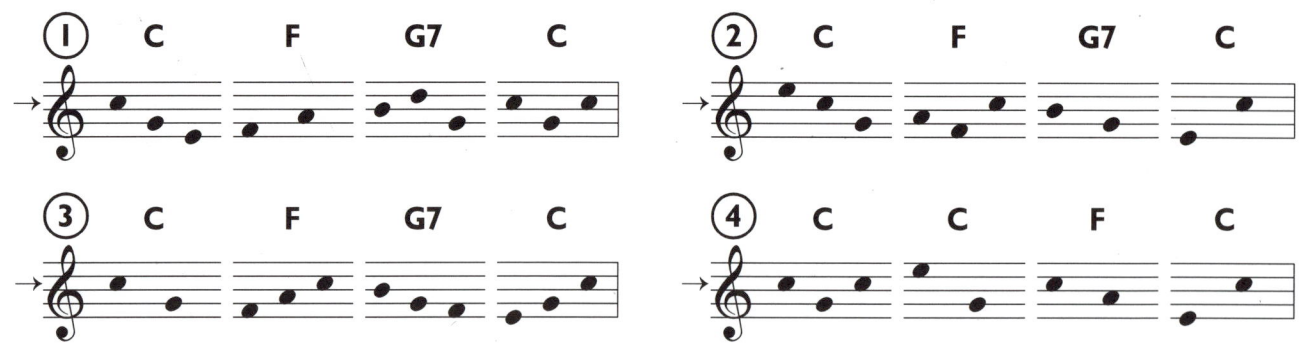

Be expressive when performing with your voice and with your instrument!

TONAL READING
TONIC, DOMINANT, AND SUBDOMINANT FUNCTIONS IN C MAJOR

1. Read the following patterns by singing them WITH TONAL SYLLABLES and by performing them on your instrument. The arrow points to DO. C indicates a TONIC major pattern; F indicates a SUBDOMINANT major pattern; and G7 indicates a DOMINANT major pattern.

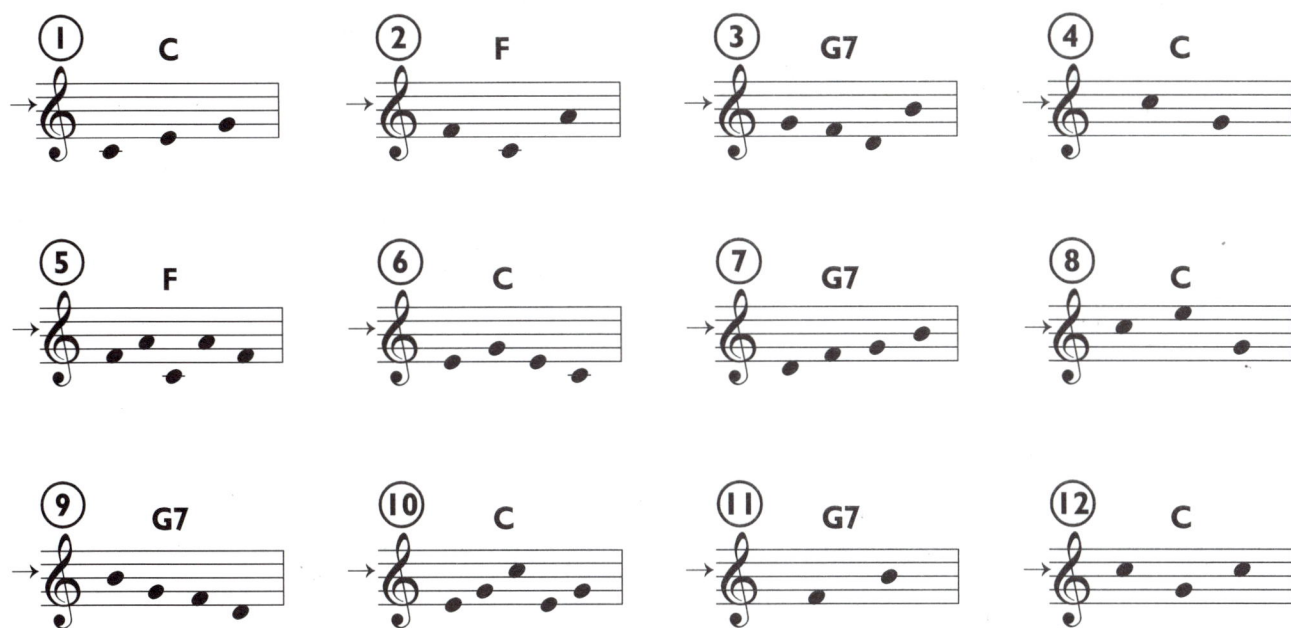

2. Read the following series of patterns by singing them WITH TONAL SYLLABLES and by performing them on your instrument. The arrow points to DO. C indicates a TONIC major pattern; F indicates a SUBDOMINANT major pattern; and G7 indicates a DOMINANT major pattern.

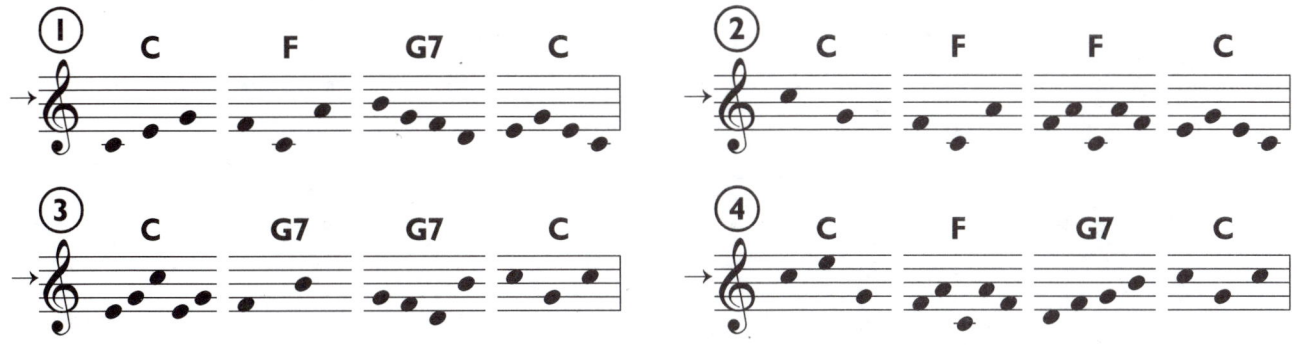

Be expressive when performing with your voice and with your instrument!

RHYTHM READING
MACROBEATS, MICROBEATS, AND RESTS IN DUPLE METER

1. Read the following patterns by chanting them WITH RHYTHM SYLLABLES and by performing them on your instrument.

   The number (2) tells how many macrobeats there are in a measure.
   The symbol (♩) indicates the kind of note that is a macrobeat.

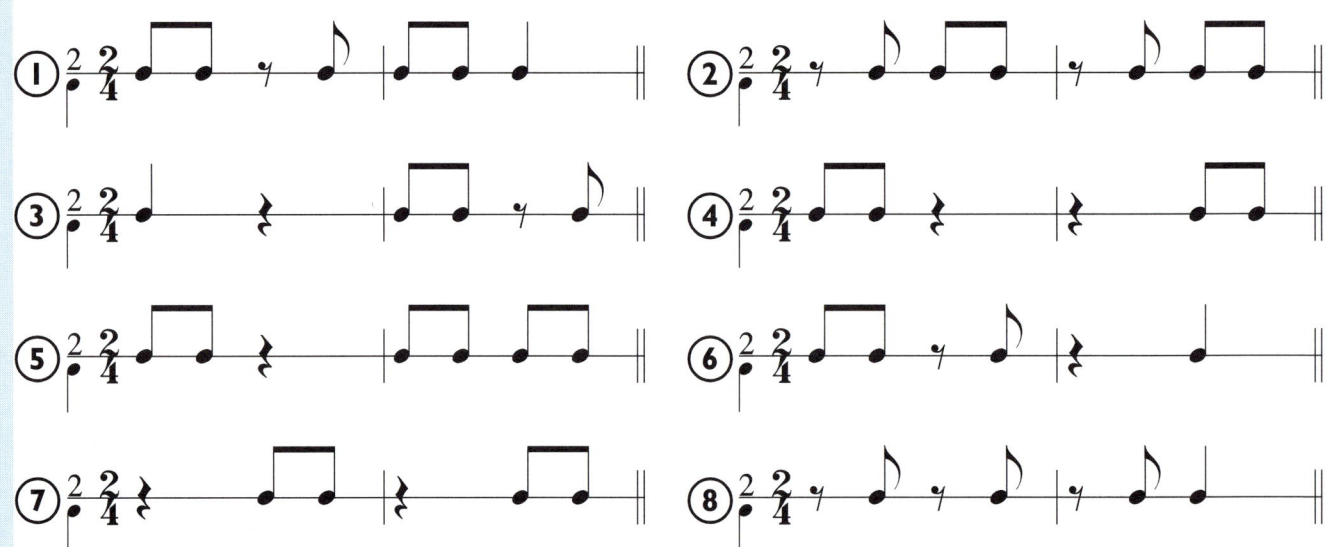

2. Read the following series of patterns by chanting them WITH RHYTHM SYLLABLES and by performing them on your instrument.

   The number (2) tells how many macrobeats there are in a measure.
   The symbol (♩) indicates the kind of note that is a macrobeat.

Be expressive when performing with your voice and with your instrument!

ENRHYTHMIC READING
MACROBEATS, MICROBEATS, AND RESTS IN DUPLE METER

1. Read the following series of patterns by chanting them WITH RHYTHM SYLLABLES and by
   performing them on your instrument. The patterns on the left (4/4) are enrhythmic (they sound the
   same, but look different) with the patterns on the right (¢).

   The numbers (4, 2) indicate how many macrobeats are in a measure.
   The symbols (♩,♩) indicate what kind of a note is a macrobeat.

Be expressive when performing with your voice and with your instrument!

LITTLE BROWN JUG

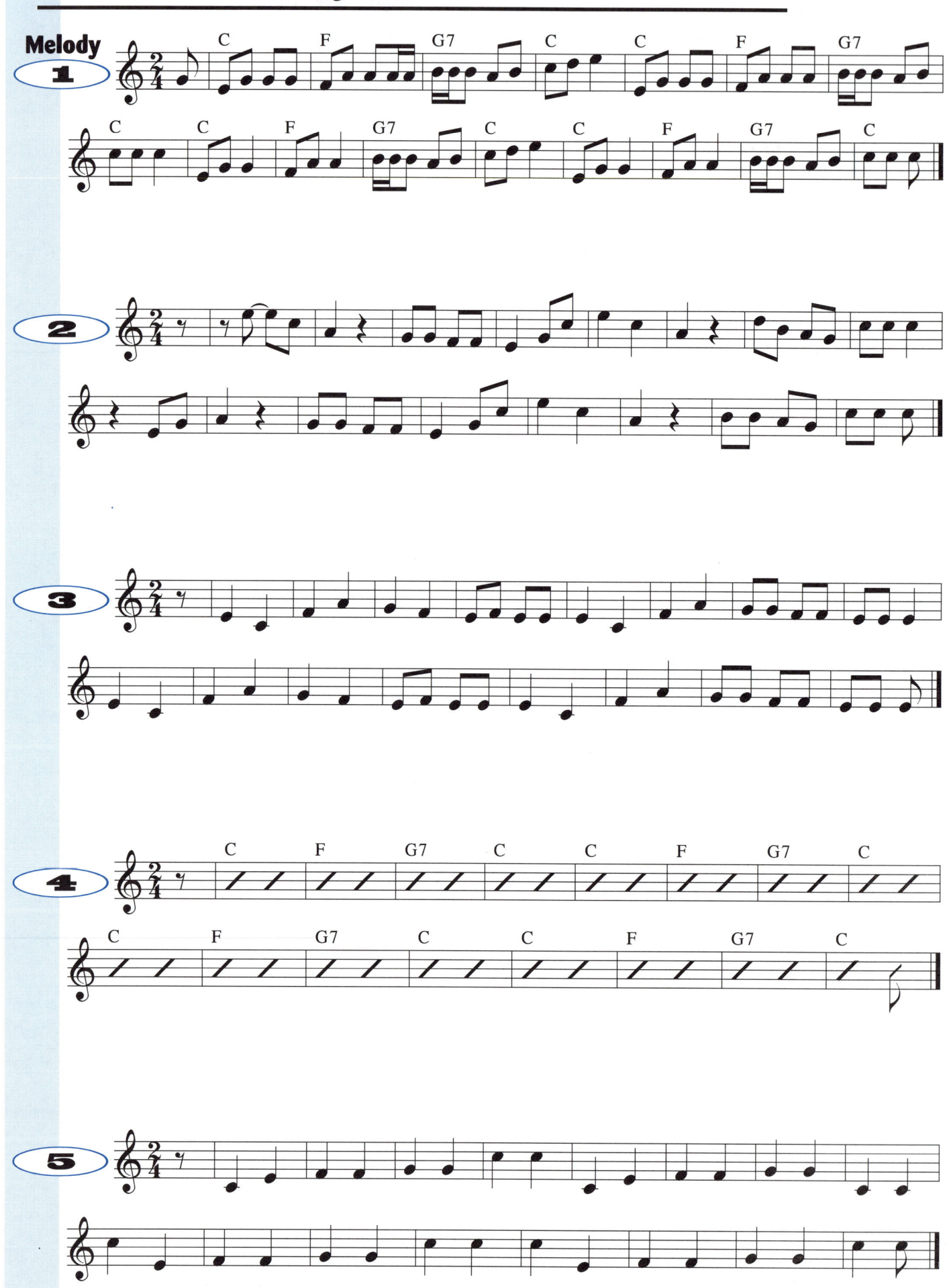

LITTLE BROWN JUG

SIMPLE GIFTS

YANKEE DOODLE

Melody 1

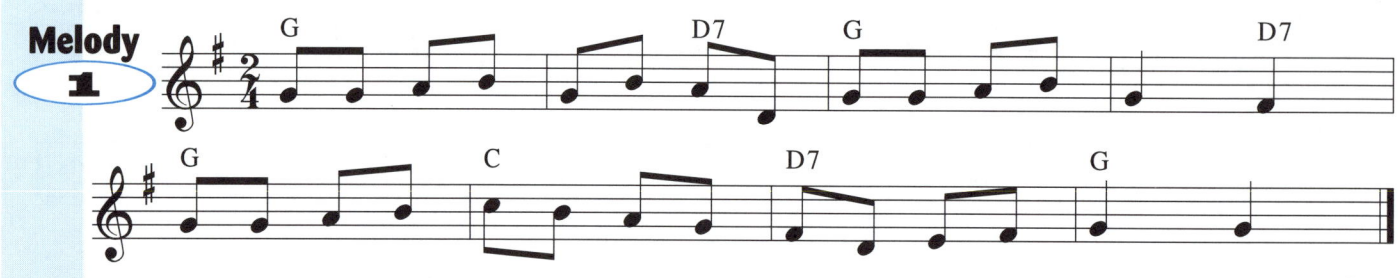

2

3

LONG, LONG AGO

Melody 1

2

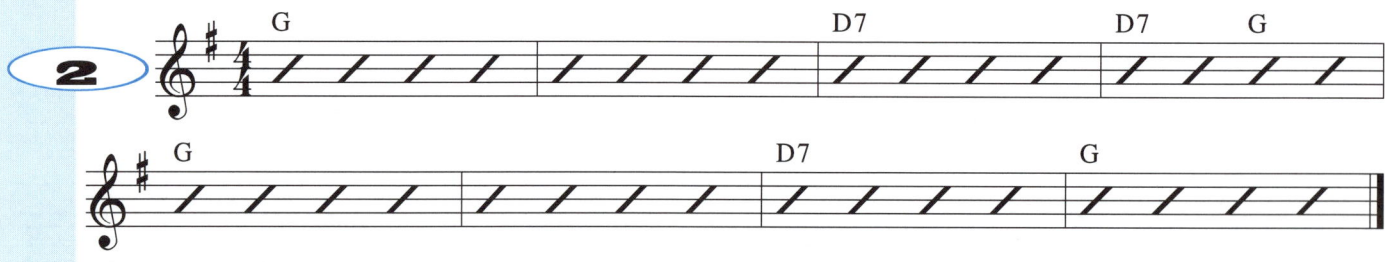

3

AMAZING GRACE

O SUSANNA

CLEMENTINE

TONAL READING
TONIC AND DOMINANT FUNCTIONS IN D MINOR

1. Read the following patterns by singing them WITH TONAL SYLLABLES and by performing them on your instrument. The arrow points to DO. Dm indicates a TONIC minor pattern; A7 indicates a DOMINANT minor pattern.

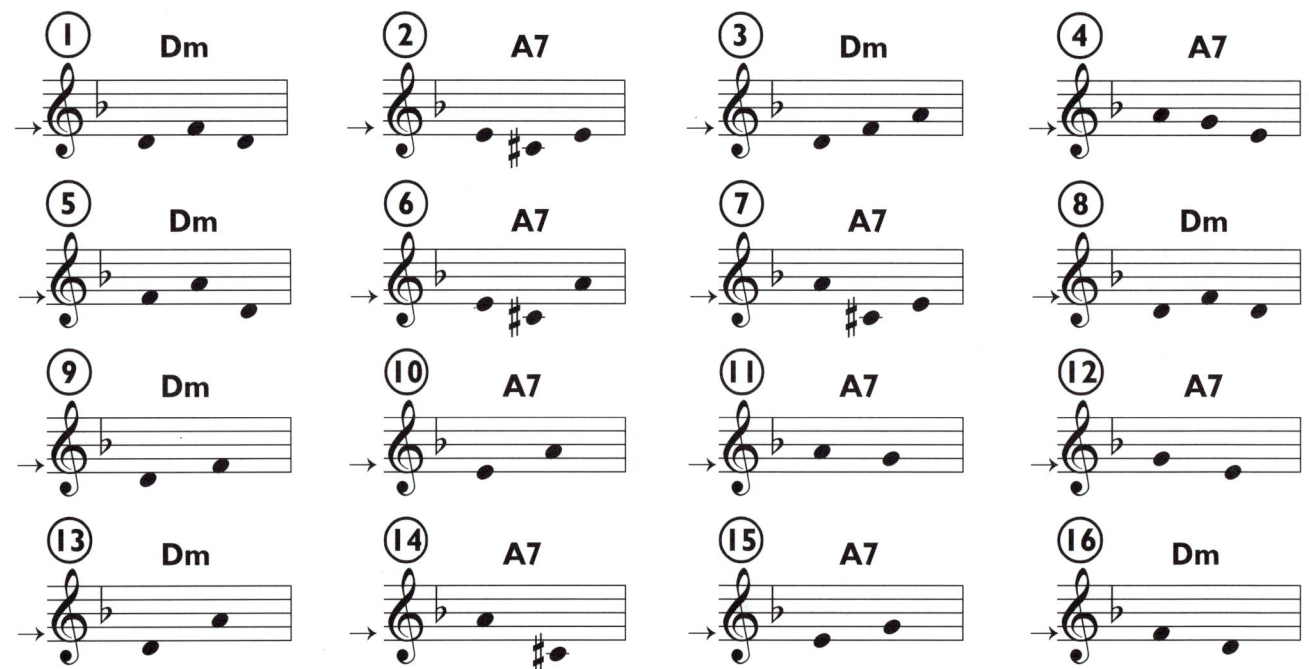

2. Read the following series of patterns by singing them WITH TONAL SYLLABLES and by performing them on your instrument. The arrow points to DO. Dm indicates a TONIC minor pattern; A7 indicates a DOMINANT minor pattern.

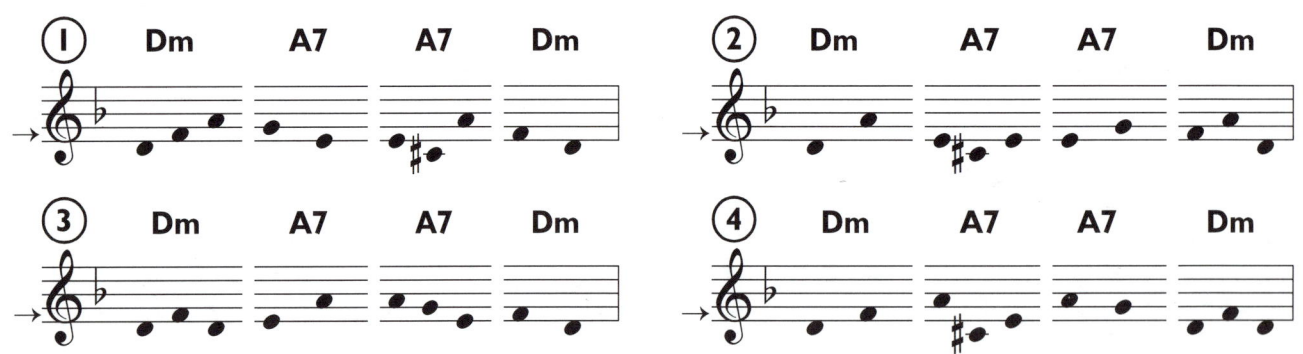

Be expressive when performing with your voice and with your instrument!

TONAL READING
TONIC, DOMINANT, AND SUBDOMINANT FUNCTIONS IN D MINOR

1. Read the following patterns by singing them WITH TONAL SYLLABLES and by performing them on your instrument. The arrow points to DO. Dm indicates a TONIC minor pattern; Gm indicates a SUBDOMINANT minor pattern; and A7 indicates a DOMINANT minor pattern.

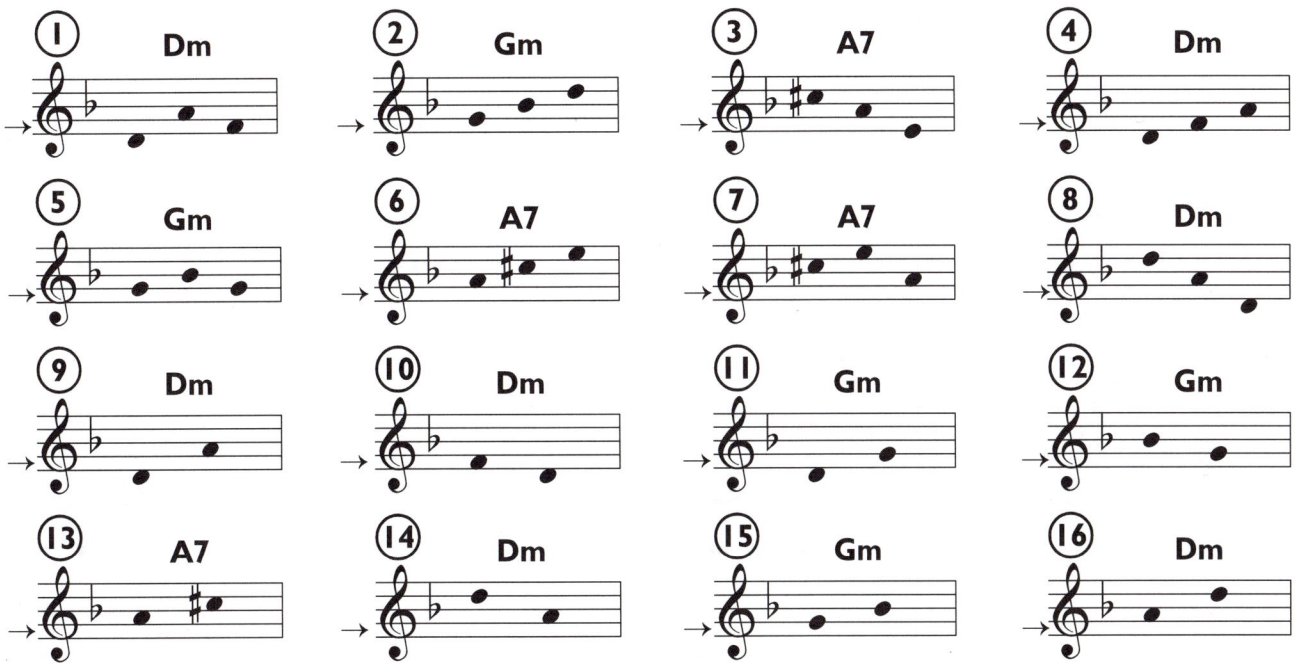

2. Read the following series of patterns by singing them WITH TONAL SYLLABLES and by performing them on your instrument. The arrow points to DO. Dm indicates a TONIC minor pattern; Gm indicates a SUBDOMINANT minor pattern; and A7 indicates a DOMINANT minor pattern.

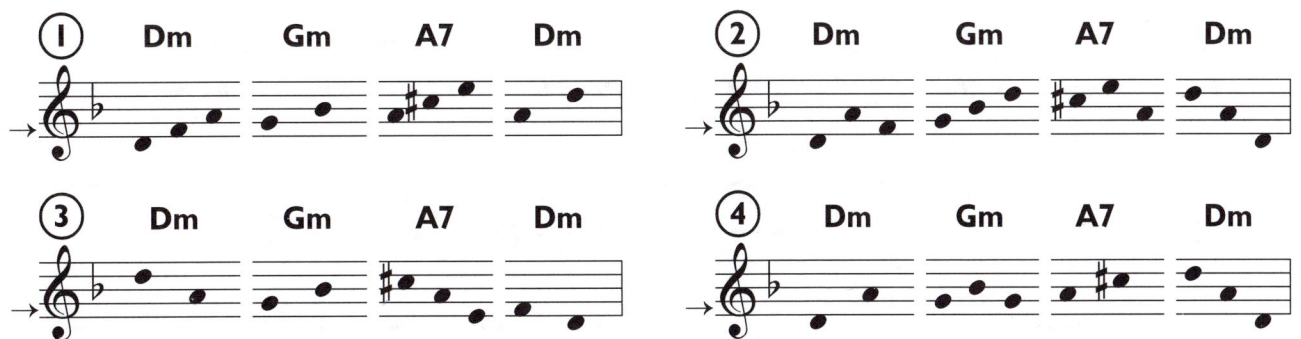

Be expressive when performing with your voice and with your instrument!

RHYTHM READING
MACROBEATS, MICROBEATS, AND RESTS IN TRIPLE METER

1. Read the following patterns by chanting them WITH RHYTHM SYLLABLES and by performing them on your instrument.

   The number (2) tells how many macrobeats there are in a measure.
   The symbol (♪·) indicates the kind of note that is a macrobeat.

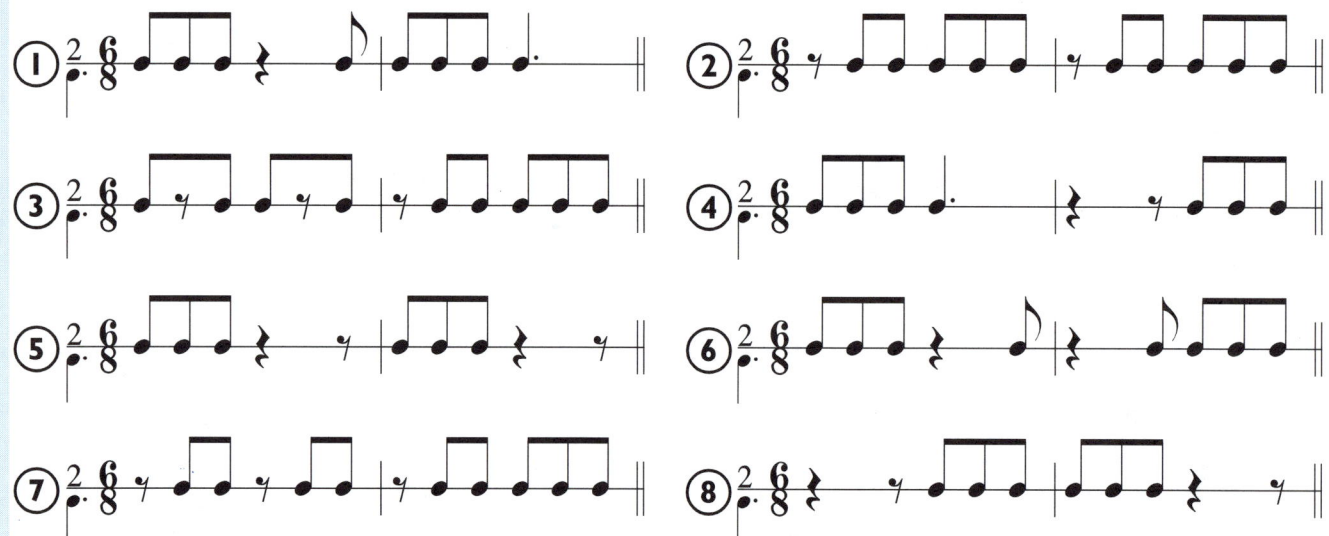

2. Read the following series of patterns by chanting them WITH RHYTHM SYLLABLES and by performing them on your instrument.

   The number (2) tells how many macrobeats there are in a measure.
   The symbol (♪·) indicates the kind of note that is a macrobeat.

Be expressive when performing with your voice and with your instrument!

ENRHYTHMIC READING
MACROBEATS, MICROBEATS, AND RESTS IN TRIPLE METER

1. Read the following patterns by chanting them WITH RHYTHM SYLLABLES and by performing them on your instrument. The patterns on the left (3/8) are enrhythmic (they sound the same, but look different) with the patterns on the right (3/4).

    The numbers (1, 1) indicate how many macrobeats are in a measure.
    The symbols (♩·,♩·) indicate what kind of a note is a macrobeat.

Be expressive when performing with your voice and with your instrument!

A LA NANITA NANA

A LA NANITA NANA

COVENTRY CAROL

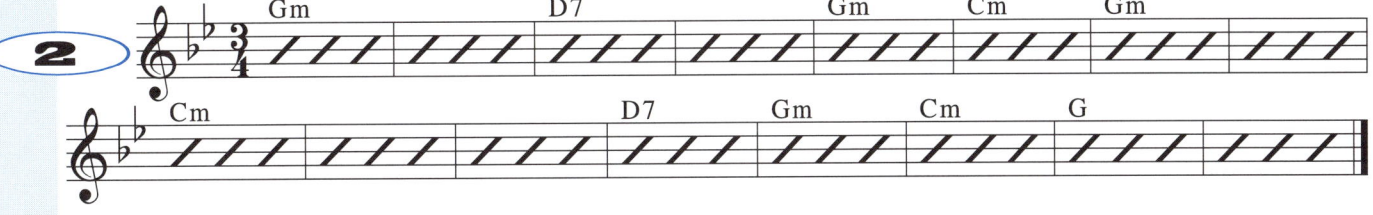

THIS OLD HAMMER

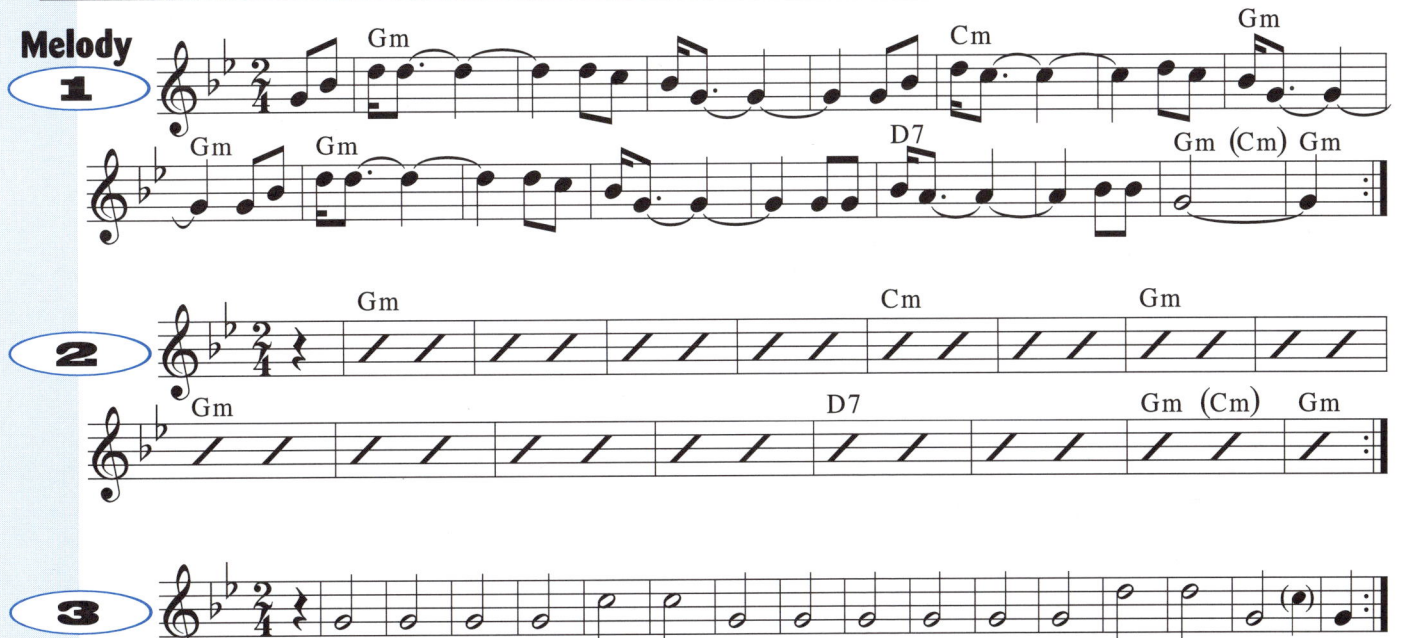

RECORDER FINGERINGS
Dorian Tonality - D is RE

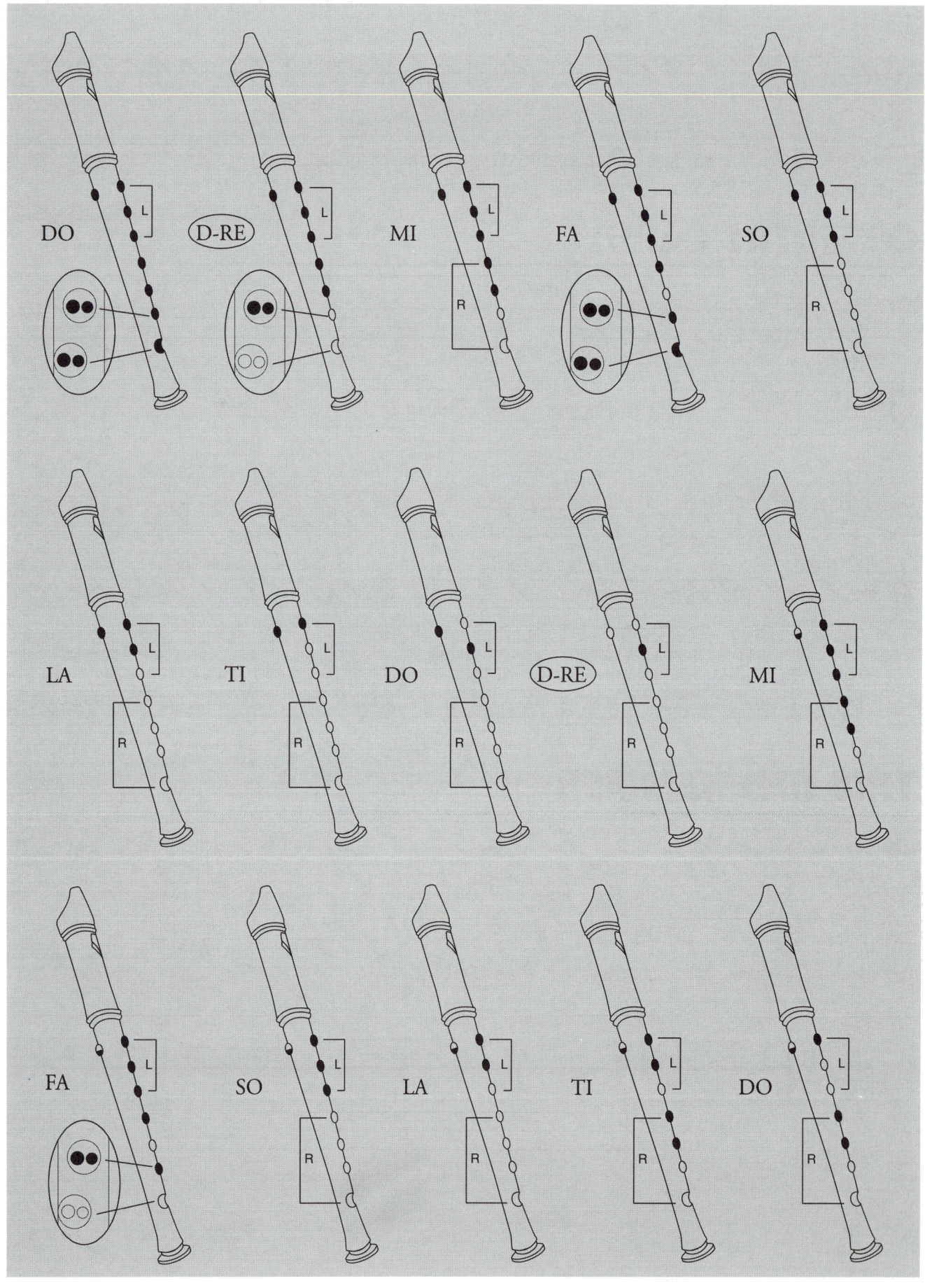

RECORDER FINGERINGS
Mixolydian Tonality - G is SO

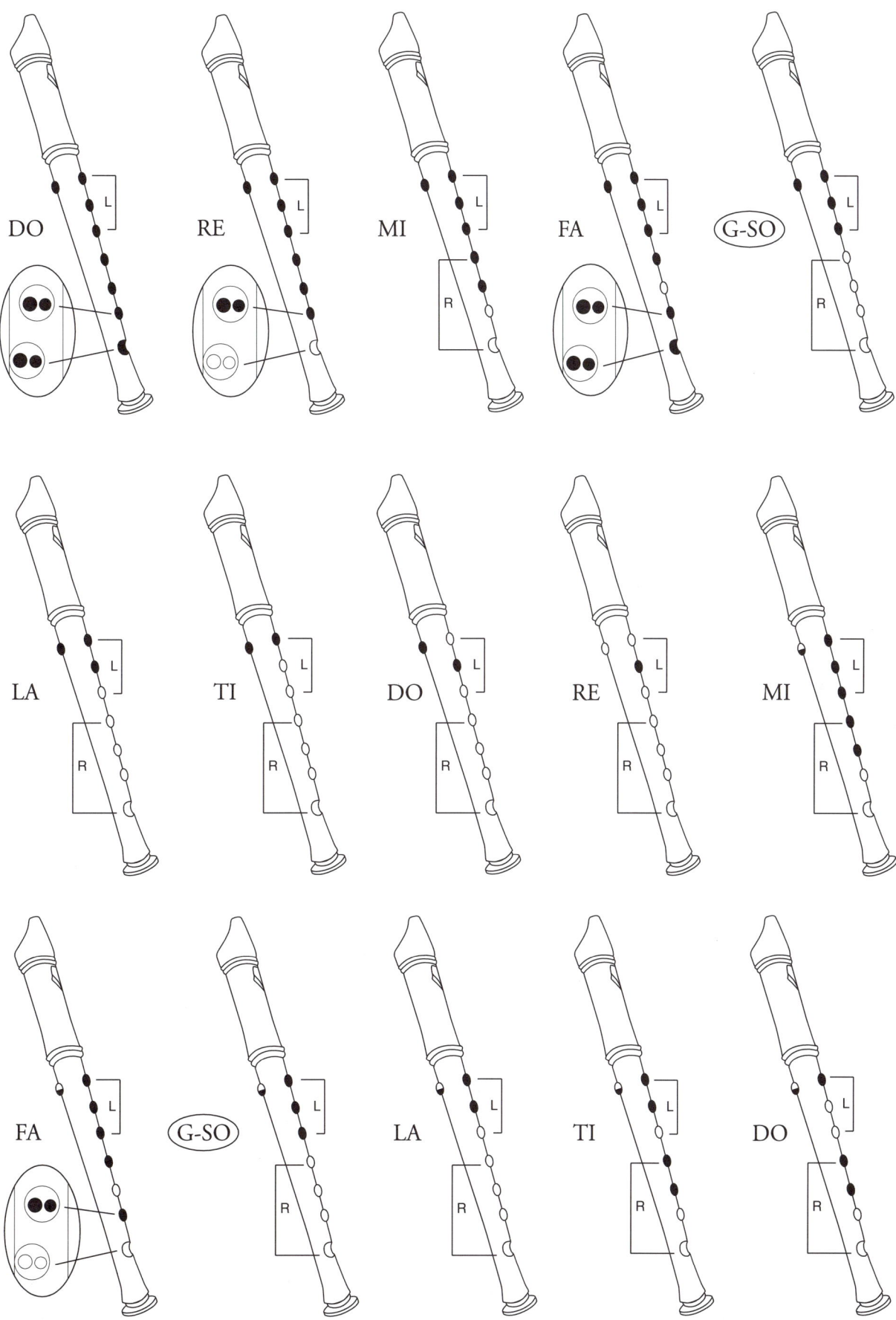

TONAL READING
TONIC AND SUBTONIC FUNCTIONS IN D DORIAN

1. Read the following patterns by singing them WITH TONAL SYLLABLES and by performing them on your instrument. The arrow points to DO. Dm indicates a TONIC Dorian pattern and C indicates a SUBTONIC Dorian pattern.

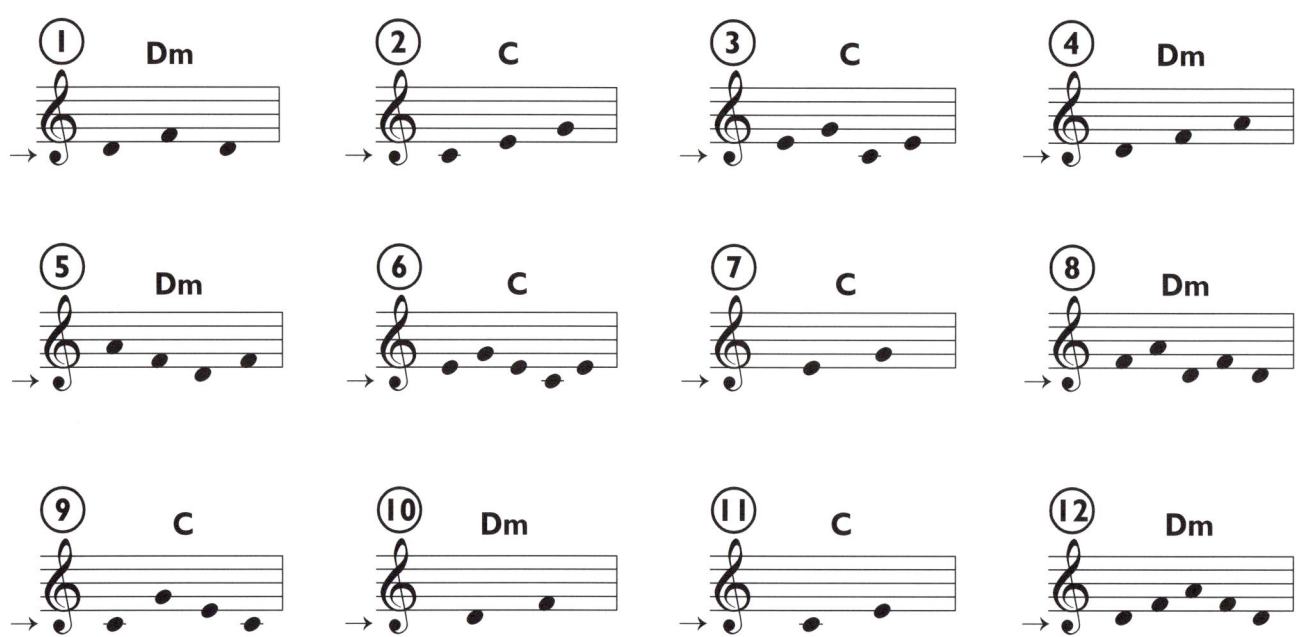

2. Read the following series of patterns by singing them WITH TONAL SYLLABLES and by performing them on your instrument. The arrow points to DO. Dm indicates a TONIC Dorian pattern and C indicates a SUBTONIC Dorian pattern.

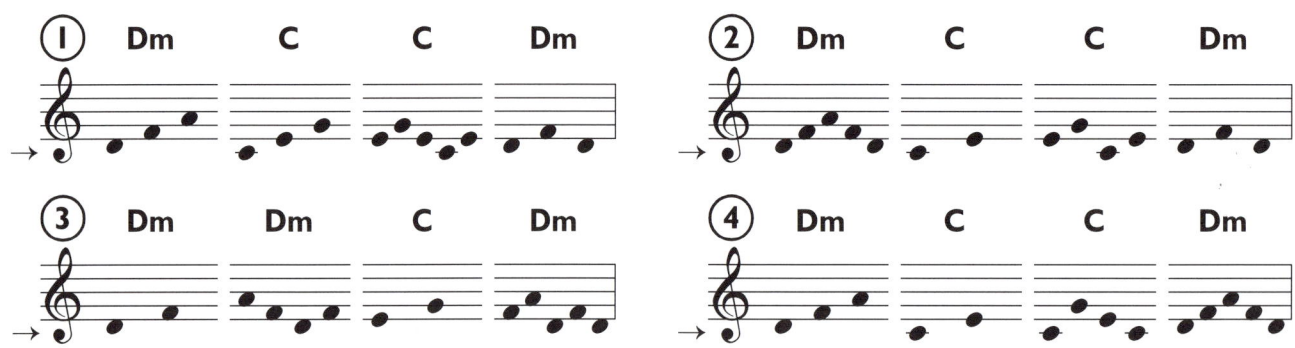

Be expressive when performing with your voice and with your instrument!

MORNING SONG

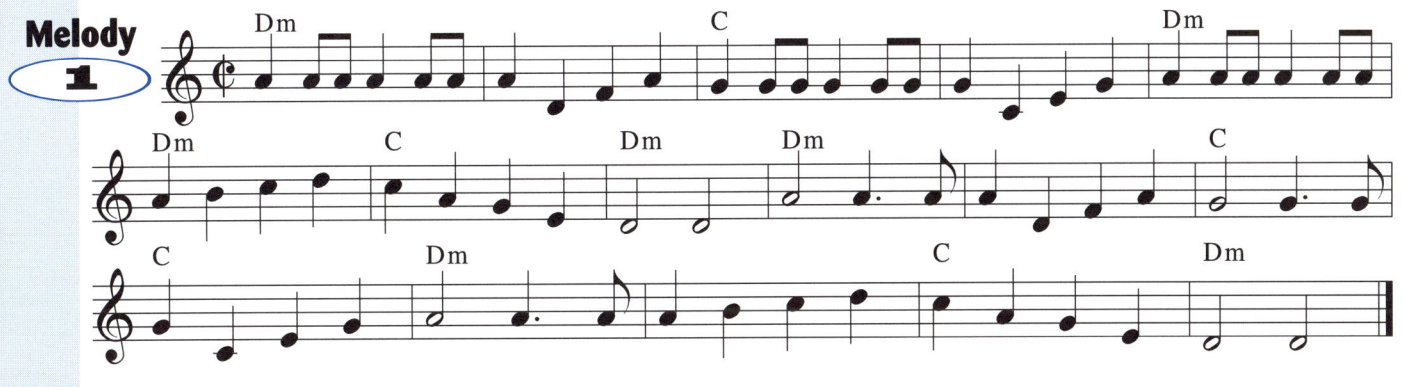

DRUNKEN SAILOR

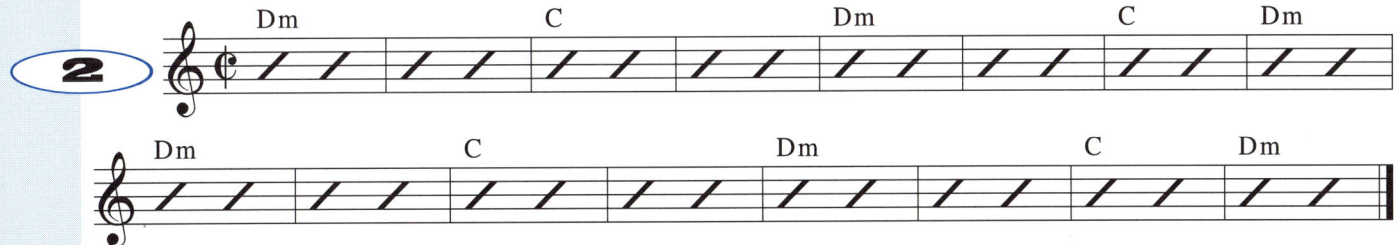

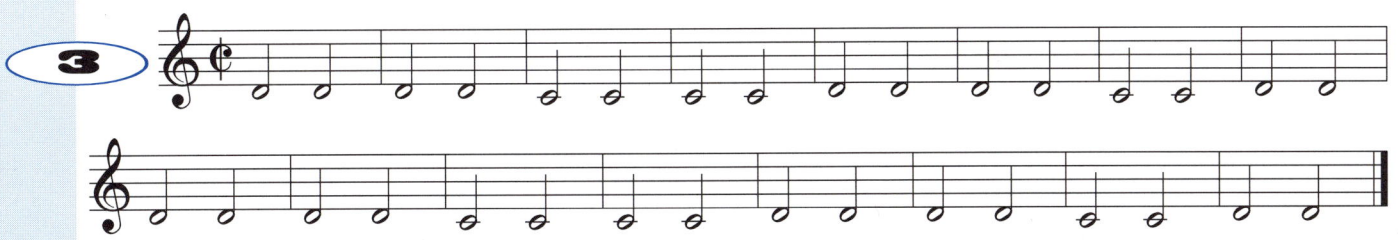

Track 70

RHYTHM READING
MACROBEATS, MICROBEATS, DIVISIONS, ELONGATIONS, RESTS, AND UPBEATS IN DUPLE METER

1. Read the following patterns by chanting them WITH RHYTHM SYLLABLES and by performing them on your instrument.

   The number (2) tells how many macrobeats there are in a measure.
   The symbol (♩) indicates the kind of note that is a macrobeat.

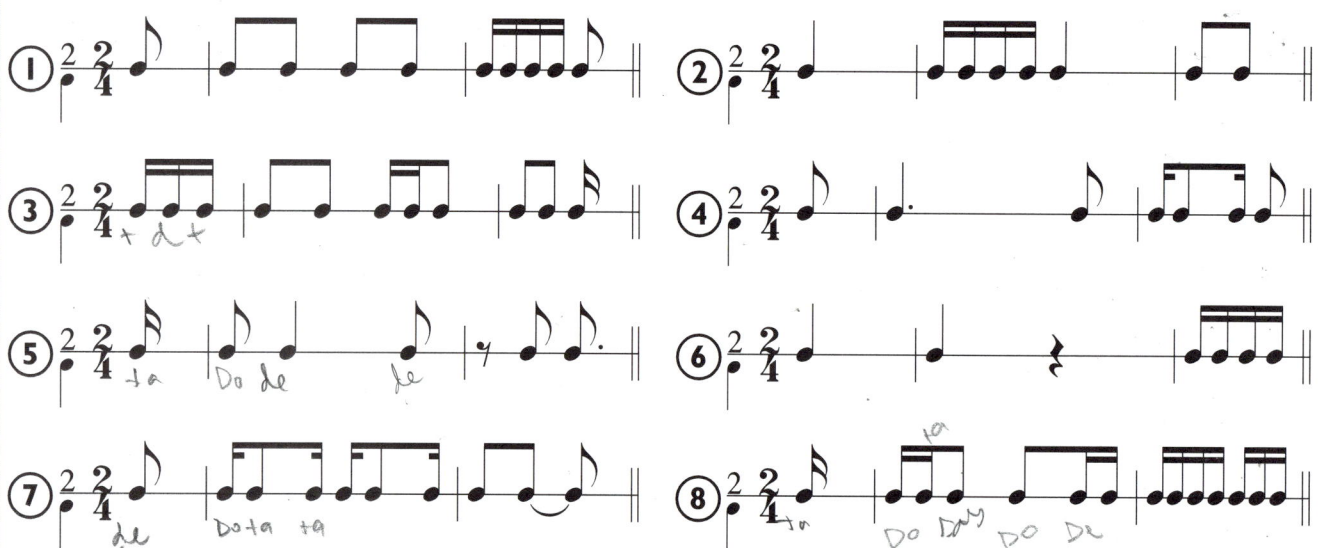

2. Read the following series of patterns by chanting them WITH RHYTHM SYLLABLES and by performing them on your instrument.

   The number (2) tells how many macrobeats there are in a measure.
   The symbol (♩) indicates the kind of note that is a macrobeat.

Be expressive when performing with your voice and with your instrument!

ENRHYTHMIC READING
MACROBEATS, MICROBEATS, DIVISIONS, ELONGATIONS,
RESTS, AND UPBEATS IN DUPLE METER

1. Read the following patterns by chanting them WITH RHYTHM SYLLABLES and by performing them on your instrument. The patterns on the left (4/4) are enrhythmic (they sound the same, but look different) with the patterns on the right (₵).

   The numbers (4, 2) indicate how many macrobeats are in a measure.
   The symbols (♩, ♩) indicate what kind of a note is a macrobeat.

Be expressive when performing with your voice and with your instrument!

TONAL READING
TONIC AND SUBTONIC FUNCTIONS IN G MIXOLYDIAN

1. Read the following patterns by singing them WITH TONAL SYLLABLES and by performing them on your instrument. The arrow points to DO. G indicates a TONIC Mixolydian pattern and F indicates a SUBTONIC Mixolydian pattern.

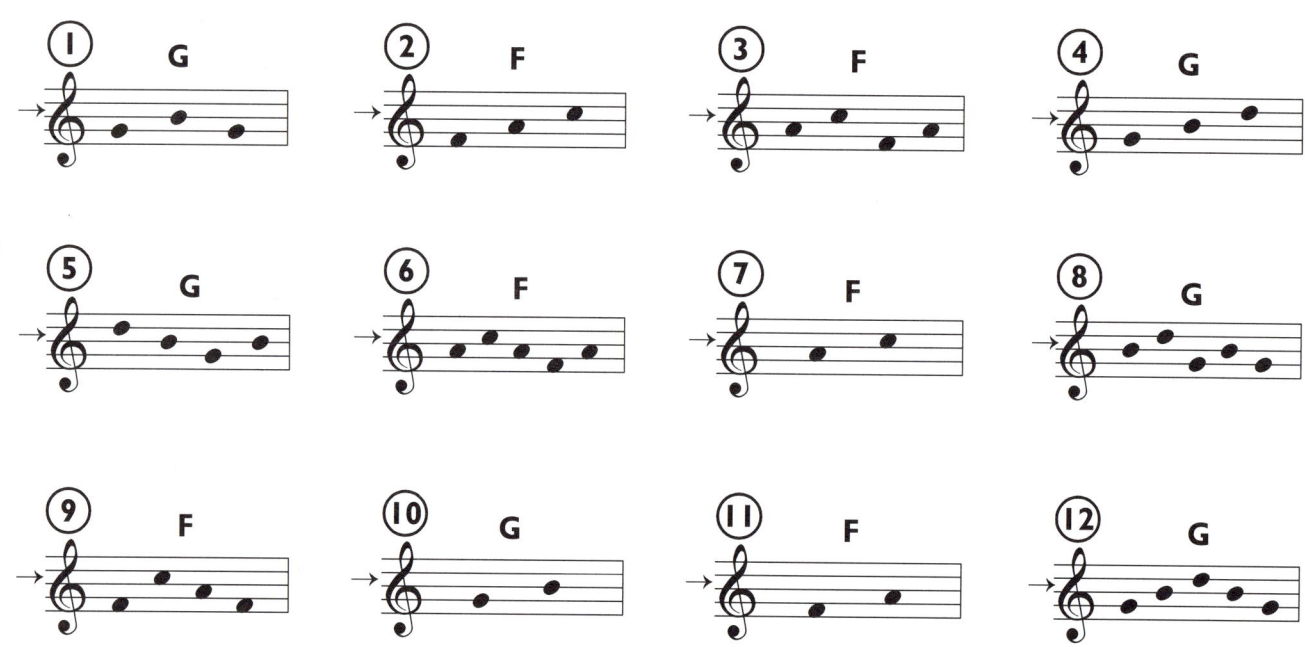

2. Read the following series of patterns by singing them WITH TONAL SYLLABLES and by performing them on your instrument. The arrow points to DO. G indicates a TONIC Mixolydian pattern and F indicates a SUBTONIC Mixolydian pattern.

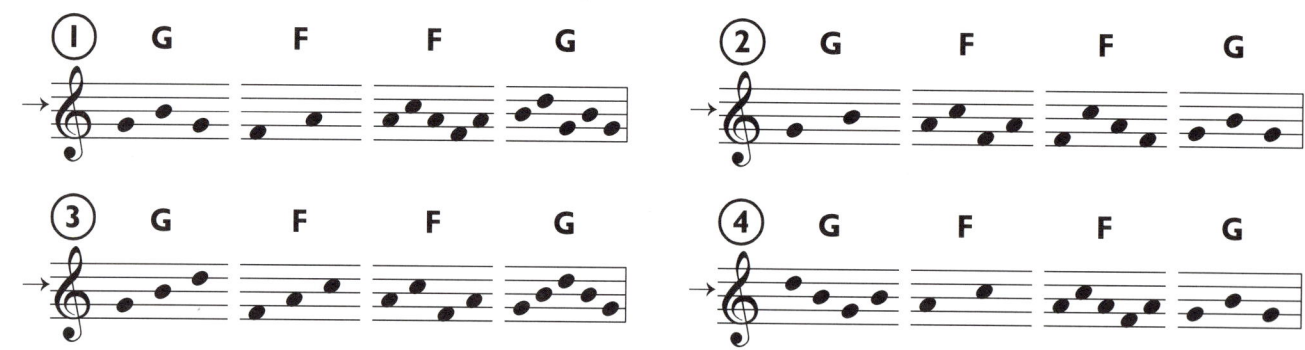

Be expressive when performing with your voice and with your instrument!

OLD JOE CLARK

RHYTHM READING
MACROBEATS, MICROBEATS, DIVISIONS, ELONGATIONS, RESTS, AND UPBEATS IN TRIPLE METER

1. Read the following patterns by chanting them WITH RHYTHM SYLLABLES and by performing them on your instrument.

   The number (2) tells how many macrobeats there are in a measure.
   The symbol (♩·) indicates the kind of note that is a macrobeat.

2. Read the following series of patterns by chanting them WITH RHYTHM SYLLABLES and by performing them on your instrument.

   The number (2) tells how many macrobeats there are in a measure.
   The symbol (♩·) indicates the kind of note that is a macrobeat.

Be expressive when performing with your voice and with your instrument!

ENRHYTHMIC READING.
MACROBEATS, MICROBEATS, DIVISIONS, ELONGATIONS,
RESTS, AND UPBEATS IN TRIPLE METER

1. Read the following patterns by chanting them WITH RHYTHM SYLLABLES and by performing them on your instrument. The patterns on the left (3/8) are enrhythmic (they sound the same, but look different) with the patterns on the right (3/4).

The numbers (1, 1) indicate how many macrobeats are in a measure.
The symbols (♩. , ♪.) indicate what kind of a note is a macrobeat.

Be expressive when performing with your voice and with your instrument!

TONAL READING
TONIC, SUBTONIC, AND SUBDOMINANT FUNCTIONS IN D DORIAN

1. Read the following patterns by singing them WITH TONAL SYLLABLES and by performing them on your instrument. The arrow points to DO. Dm indicates a TONIC Dorian pattern; C indicates a SUBTONIC Dorian pattern; and G indicates a SUBDOMINANT Dorian pattern.

2. Read the following series of patterns by singing them WITH TONAL SYLLABLES and by performing them on your instrument. The arrow points to DO. Dm indicates a TONIC Dorian pattern; C indicates a SUBTONIC Dorian pattern; and G indicates a SUBDOMINANT Dorian pattern.

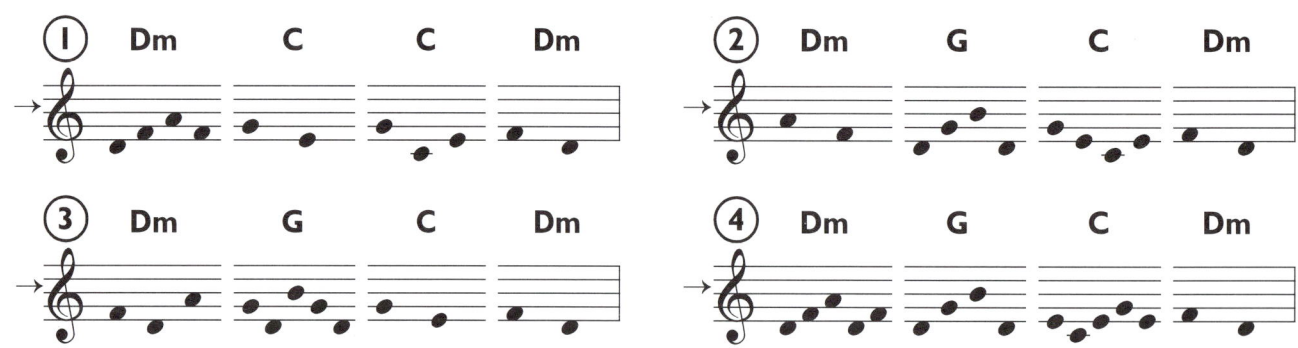

Be expressive when performing with your voice and with your instrument!

GREENSLEEVES

RHYTHM READING
MACROBEATS, MICROBEATS, DIVISIONS, ELONGATIONS, RESTS, UPBEATS, AND TIES IN DUPLE METER

1. Read the following patterns by chanting them WITH RHYTHM SYLLABLES and by performing them on your instrument.

   The number (2) tells how many macrobeats there are in a measure.
   The symbol (♩) indicates the kind of note that is a macrobeat.

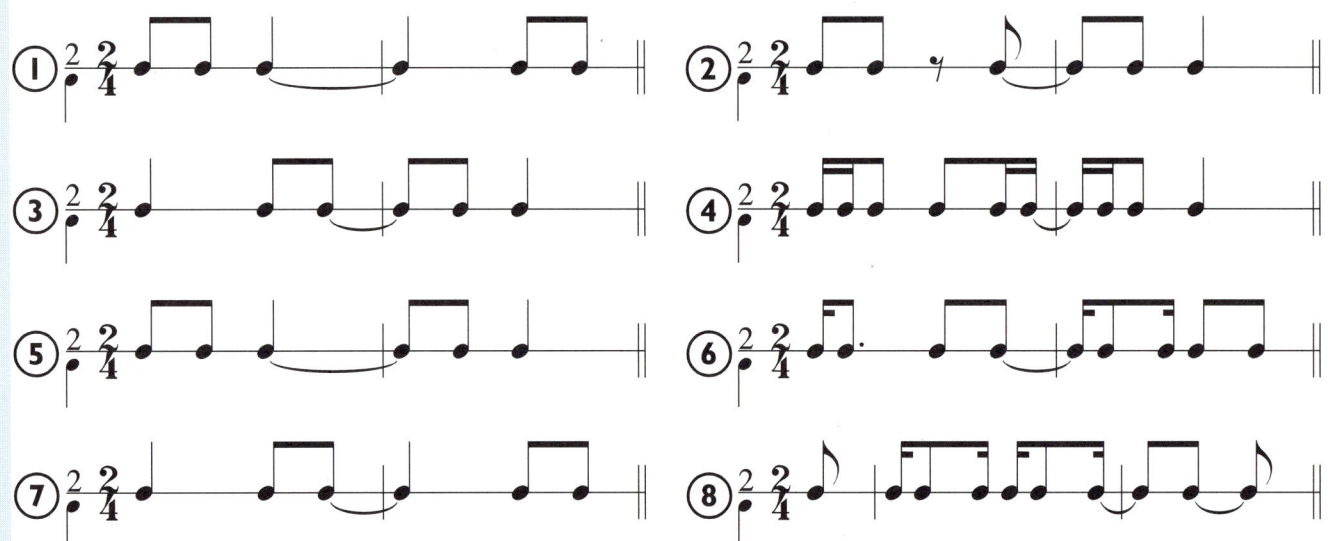

2. Read the following series of patterns by chanting them WITH RHYTHM SYLLABLES and by performing them on your instrument.

   The number (2) tells how many macrobeats there are in a measure.
   The symbol (♩) indicates the kind of note that is a macrobeat.

Be expressive when performing with your voice and with your instrument!

ENRHYTHMIC READING
MACROBEATS, MICROBEATS, DIVISIONS, ELONGATIONS, RESTS, UPBEATS, AND TIES IN DUPLE METER

1. Read the following patterns by chanting them WITH RHYTHM SYLLABLES and by performing them on your instrument. The patterns on the left (4/4) are enrhythmic (they sound the same, but look different) with the patterns on the right (¢).

The numbers (4, 2) indicate how many macrobeats are in a measure.
The symbols (♩,♩) indicate what kind of a note is a macrobeat.

Be expressive when performing with your voice and with your instrument!

TONAL READING
TONIC, SUBTONIC, AND SUBDOMINANT FUNCTIONS IN G MIXOLYDIAN

1. Read the following patterns by singing them WITH TONAL SYLLABLES and by performing them on your instrument. The arrow points to DO. G indicates a TONIC Mixolydian pattern; F indicates a SUBTONIC Mixolydian pattern; and C indicates a SUBDOMINANT Mixolydian pattern.

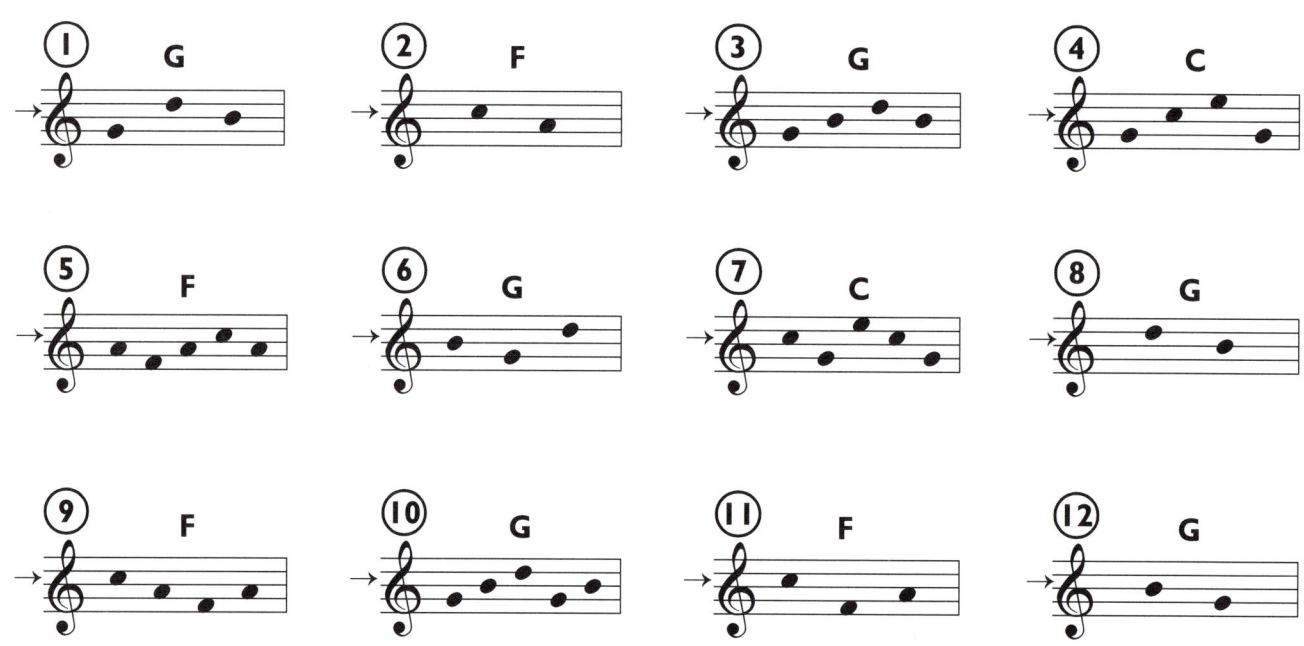

2. Read the following series of patterns by singing them WITH TONAL SYLLABLES and by performing them on your instrument. The arrow points to DO. G indicates a TONIC Mixolydian pattern; F indicates a SUBTONIC Mixolydian pattern; and C indicates a SUBDOMINANT Mixolydian pattern.

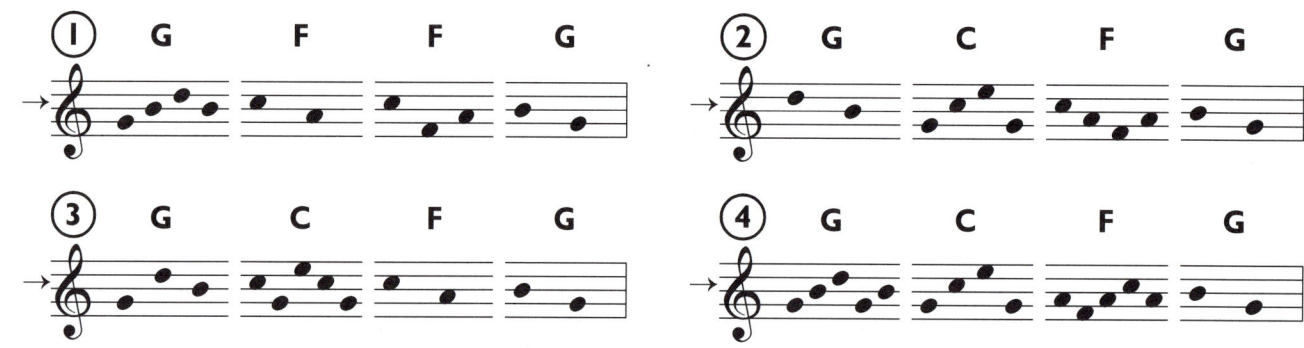

Be expressive when performing with your voice and with your instrument!

I'M GONNA PUT ON MY WALKIN' SHOES

RHYTHM READING
MACROBEATS, MICROBEATS, DIVISIONS, ELONGATIONS, RESTS, UPBEATS, AND TIES IN TRIPLE METER

1. Read the following patterns by chanting them WITH RHYTHM SYLLABLES and by performing them on your instrument.

    The number (2) tells how many macrobeats there are in a measure.
    The symbol ($\bullet\cdot$) indicates the kind of note that is a macrobeat.

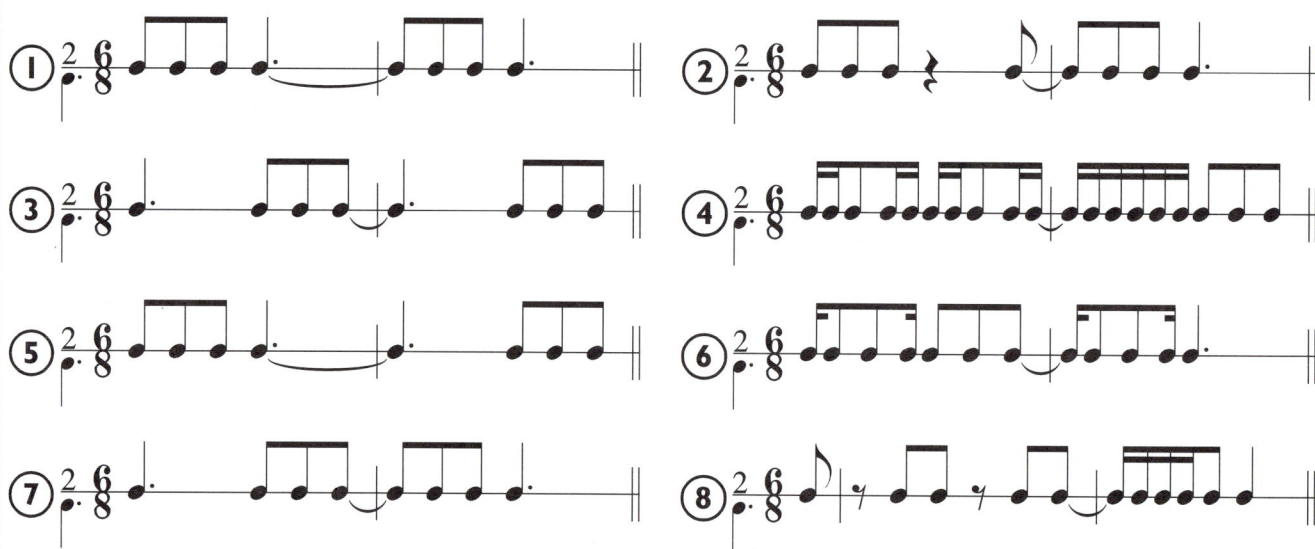

2. Read the following series of patterns by chanting them WITH RHYTHM SYLLABLES and by performing them on your instrument.

    The number (2) tells how many macrobeats there are in a measure.
    The symbol ($\bullet\cdot$) indicates the kind of note that is a macrobeat.

Be expressive when performing with your voice and with your instrument!

ENRHYTHMIC READING
MACROBEATS, MICROBEATS, DIVISIONS, ELONGATIONS, RESTS, UPBEATS, AND TIES IN TRIPLE METER

1. Read the following patterns by chanting them WITH RHYTHM SYLLABLES and by performing them on your instrument. The patterns on the left (3/8) are enrhythmic (they sound the same, but look different) with the patterns on the right (3/4).

The numbers (1, 1) indicate how many macrobeats are in a measure.
The symbols (♩. , ♩·) indicate what kind of a note is a macrobeat.

Be expressive when performing with your voice and with your instrument!

RHYTHM READING
MACROBEATS AND MICROBEATS IN UNUSUAL PAIRED METER

1. Read the following patterns by chanting them WITH RHYTHM SYLLABLES and by performing them on your instrument.

    The number (2) tells how many macrobeats there are in a measure.
    The symbols (♩· ♩) indicate the kind of notes that are macrobeats.

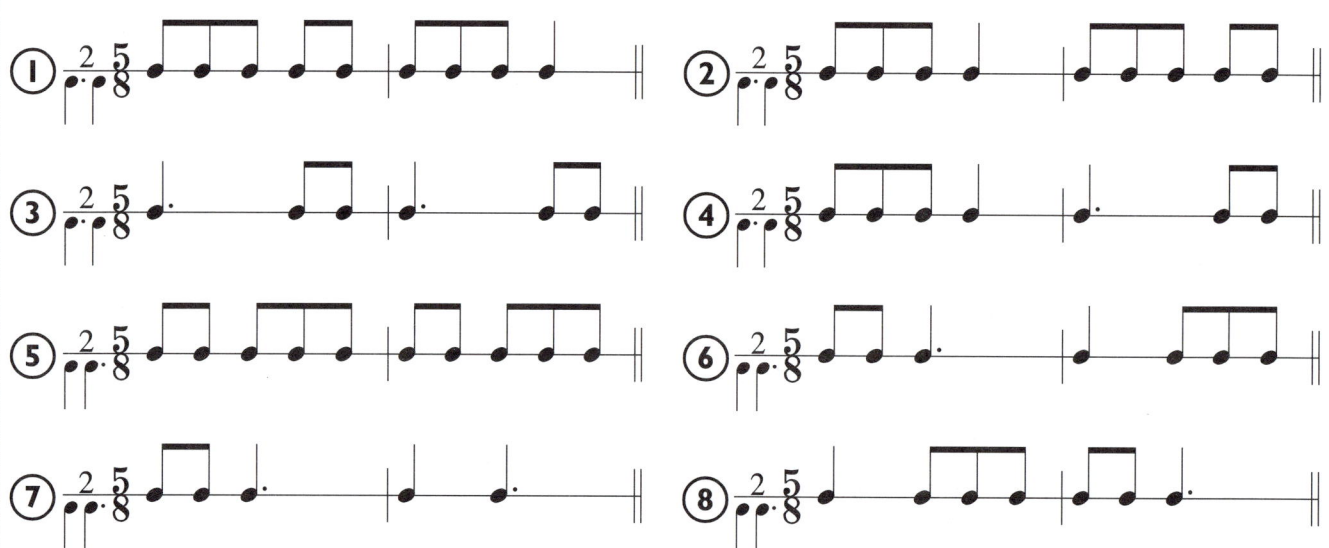

2. Read the following series of patterns by chanting them WITH RHYTHM SYLLABLES and by performing them on your instrument.

    The number (2) tells how many macrobeats there are in a measure.
    The symbols (♩· ♩) indicate the kind of notes that are macrobeats.

Be expressive when performing with your voice and with your instrument!

RHYTHM READING
MACROBEATS, MICROBEATS, AND DIVISIONS IN UNUSUAL PAIRED METER

1. Read the following patterns by chanting them WITH RHYTHM SYLLABLES and by performing them on your instrument.

   The number (2) tells how many macrobeats there are in a measure.
   The symbols (♪· ♪) indicate the kind of notes that are macrobeats.

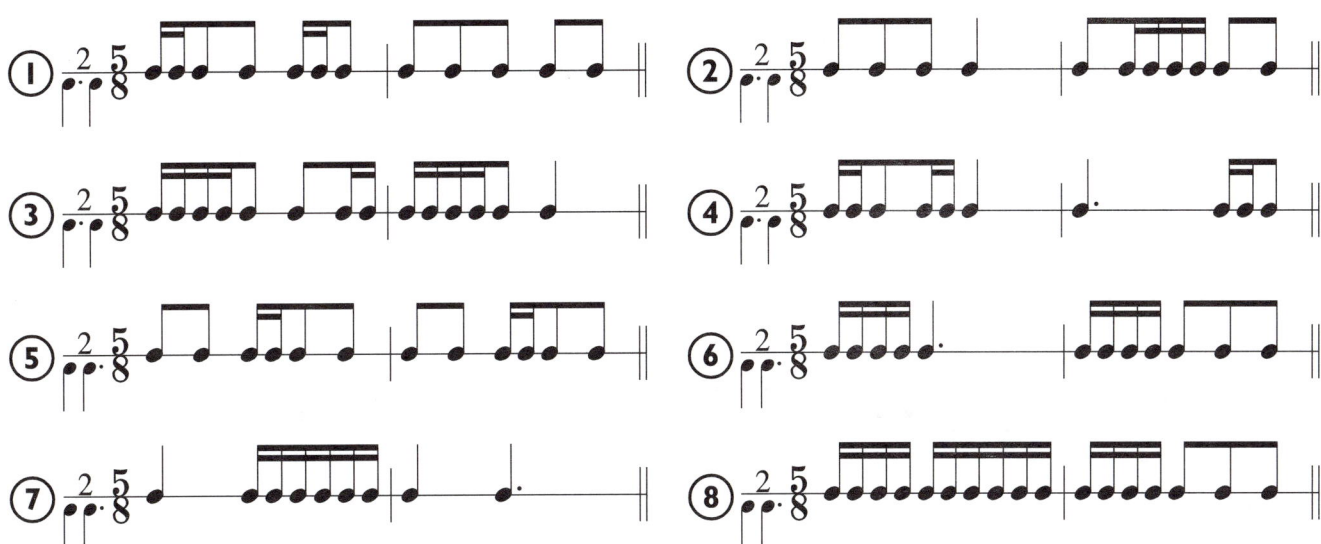

2. Read the following series of patterns by chanting them WITH RHYTHM SYLLABLES and by performing them on your instrument.

   The number (2) tells how many macrobeats there are in a measure.
   The symbols (♪· ♪) indicate the kind of notes that are macrobeats.

Be expressive when performing with your voice and with your instrument!

WINTER DAY

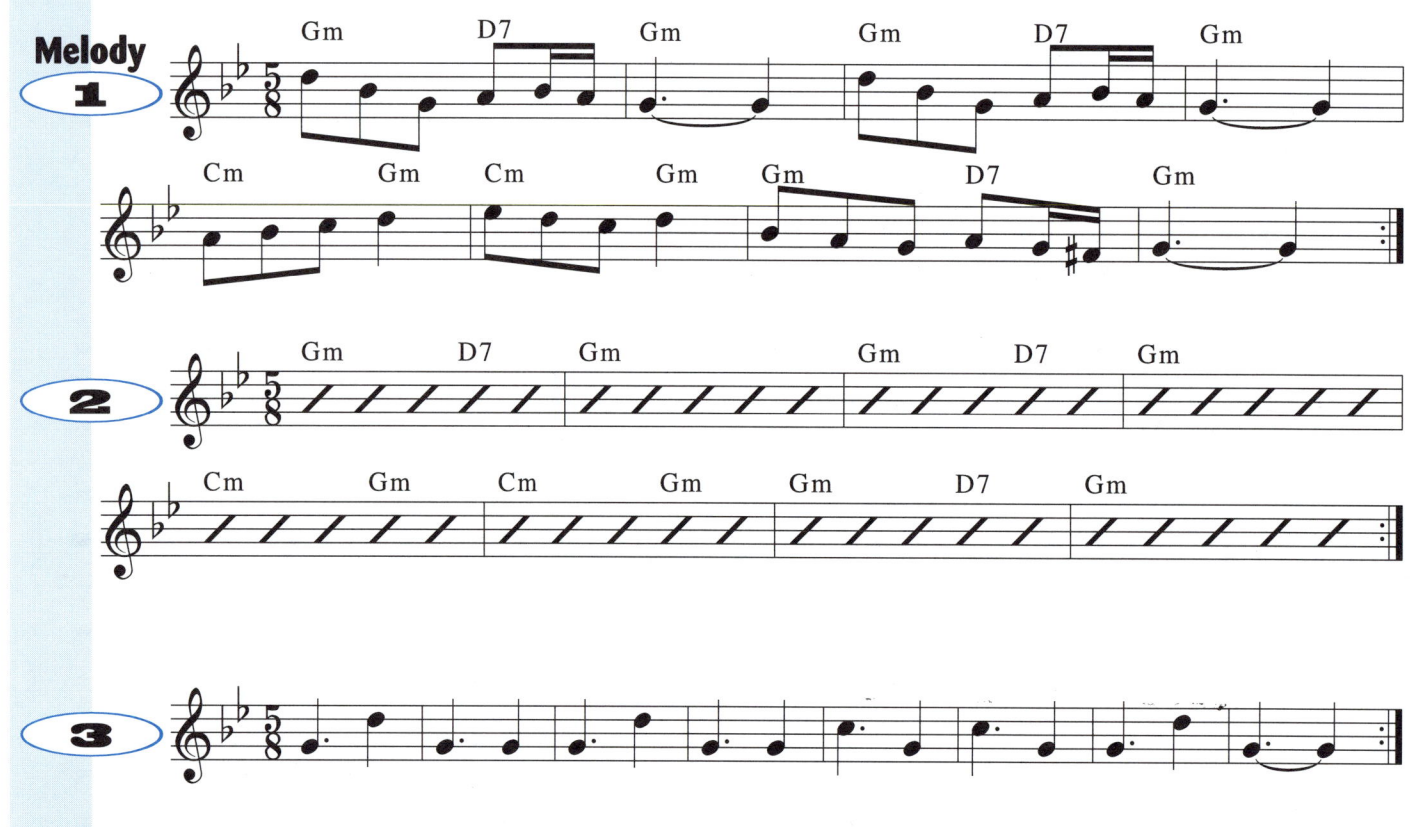

PEASANT DANCE

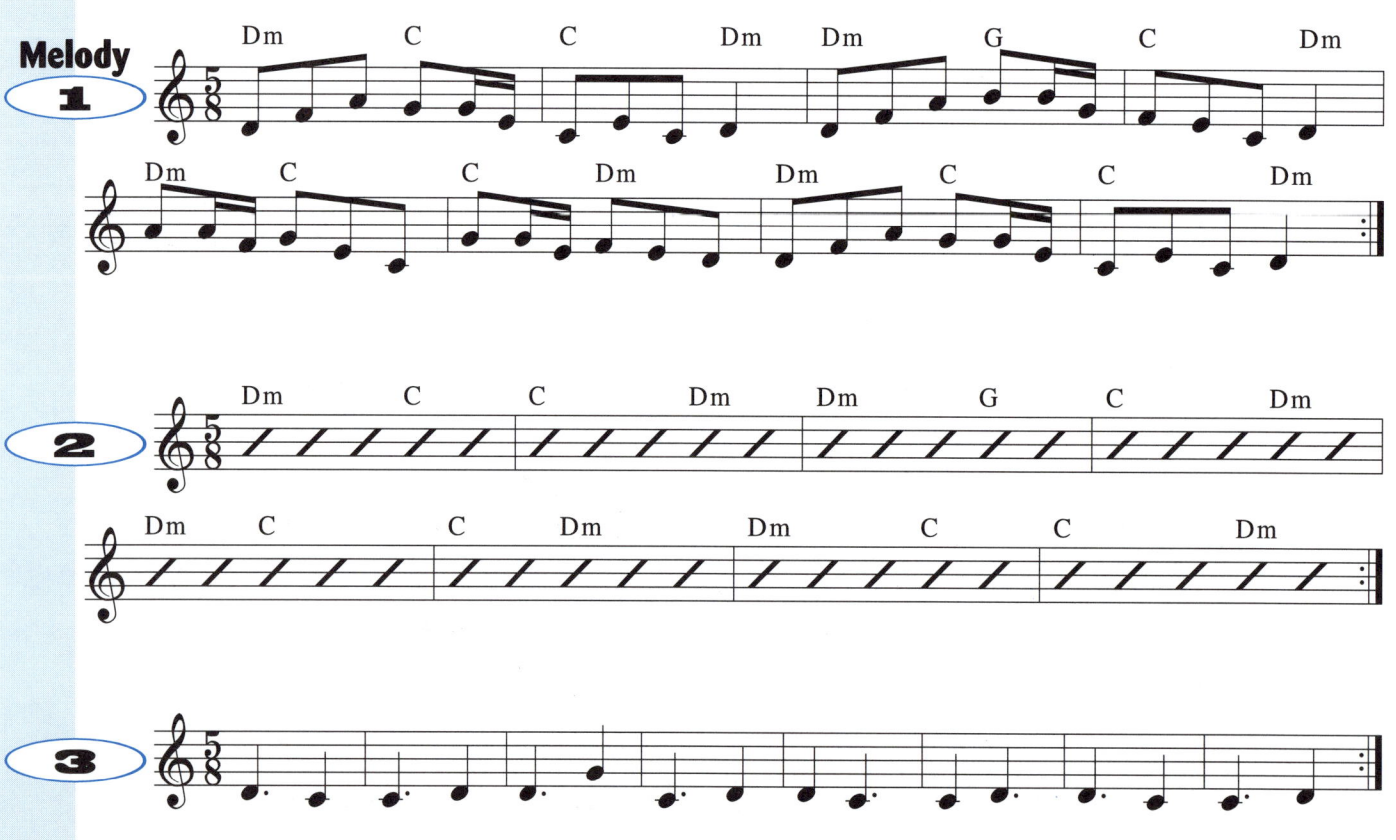

RHYTHM READING
MACROBEATS AND MICROBEATS IN UNUSUAL UNPAIRED METER

1. Read the following patterns by chanting them WITH RHYTHM SYLLABLES and by performing them on your instrument.

    The number (3) tells how many macrobeats there are in a measure.
    The symbols (♩· ♩) indicate the kind of notes that are macrobeats.

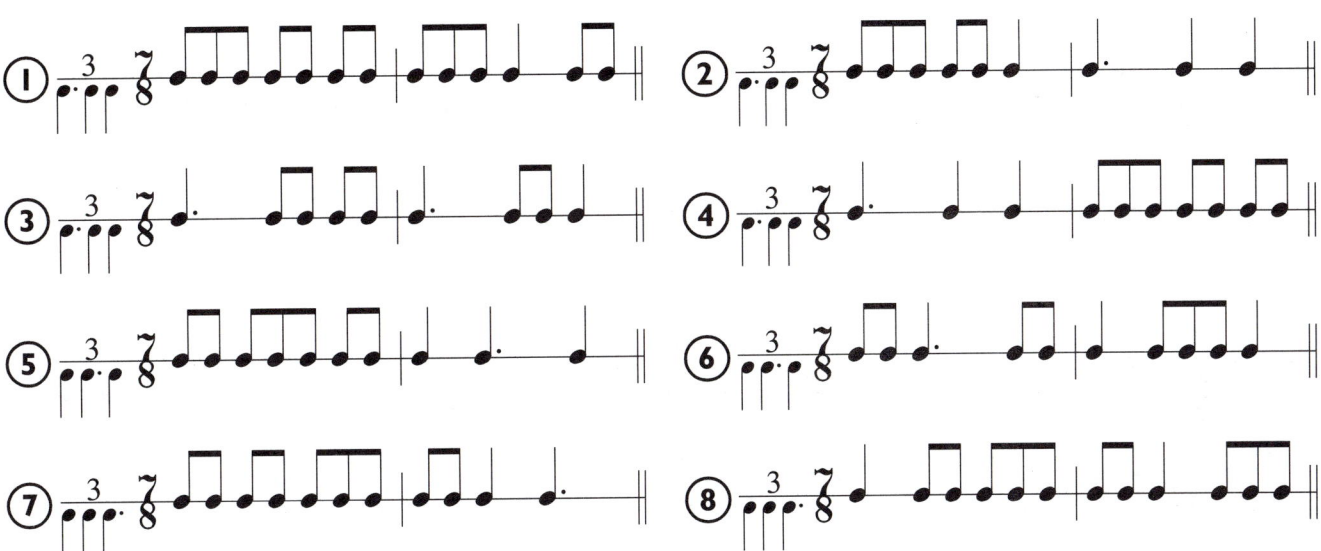

2. Read the following series of patterns by chanting them WITH RHYTHM SYLLABLES and by performing them on your instrument.

    The number (3) tells how many macrobeats there are in a measure.
    The symbols (♩· ♩) indicate the kind of notes that are macrobeats.

Be expressive when performing with your voice and with your instrument!

YERAKINA

Melody 1

Melody 2

Melody 3

THREE YOUNG MEN FROM VOLOS

Melody 1

Melody 2

Melody 3

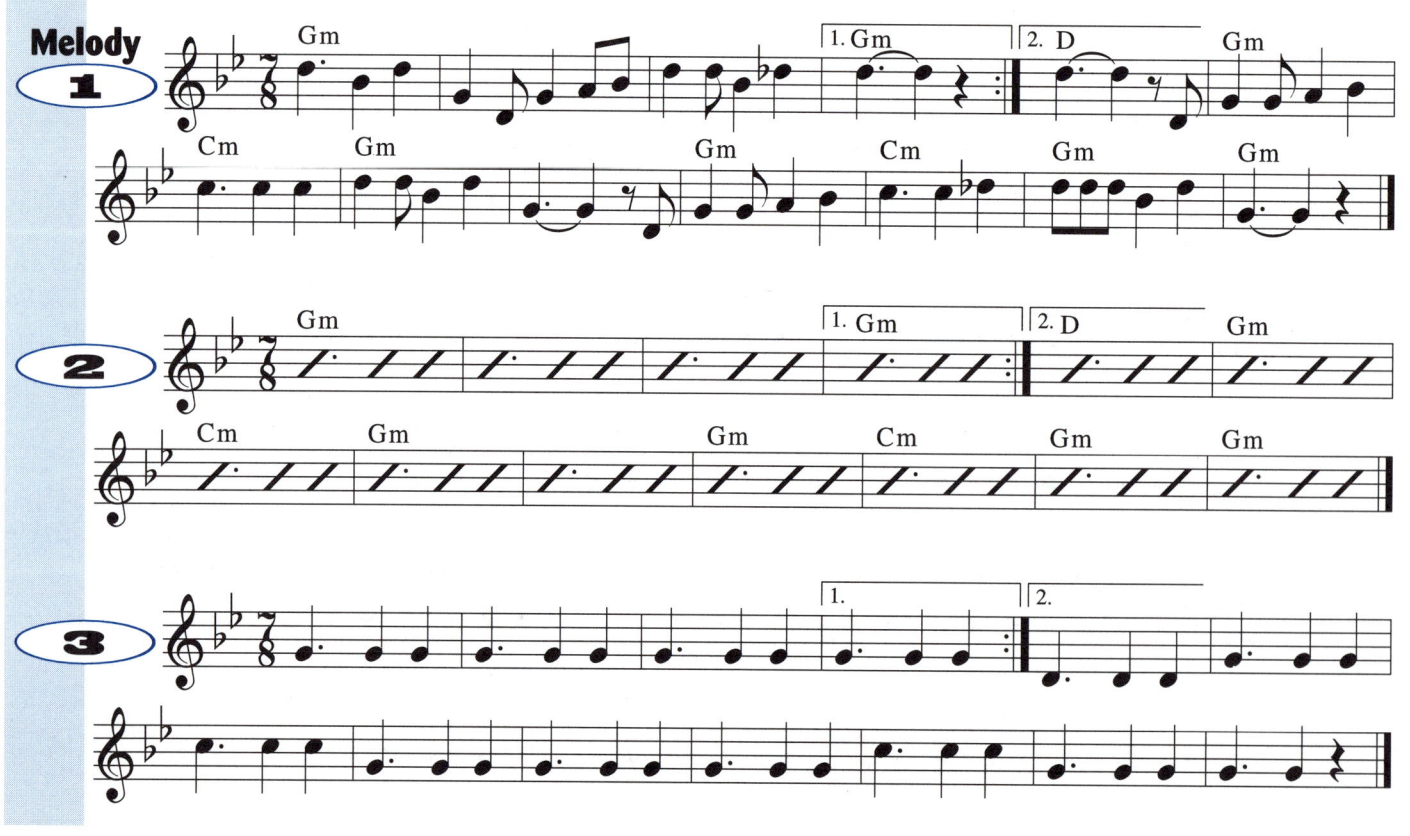

RHYTHM READING
MACROBEATS AND MICROBEATS IN COMBINED METER

1. Read the following patterns by chanting them WITH RHYTHM SYLLABLES and by performing them on your instrument.

   The number (2) tells how many macrobeats there are in a measure.
   The symbol (♪, ♪·) indicates the kind of note that is a macrobeat.

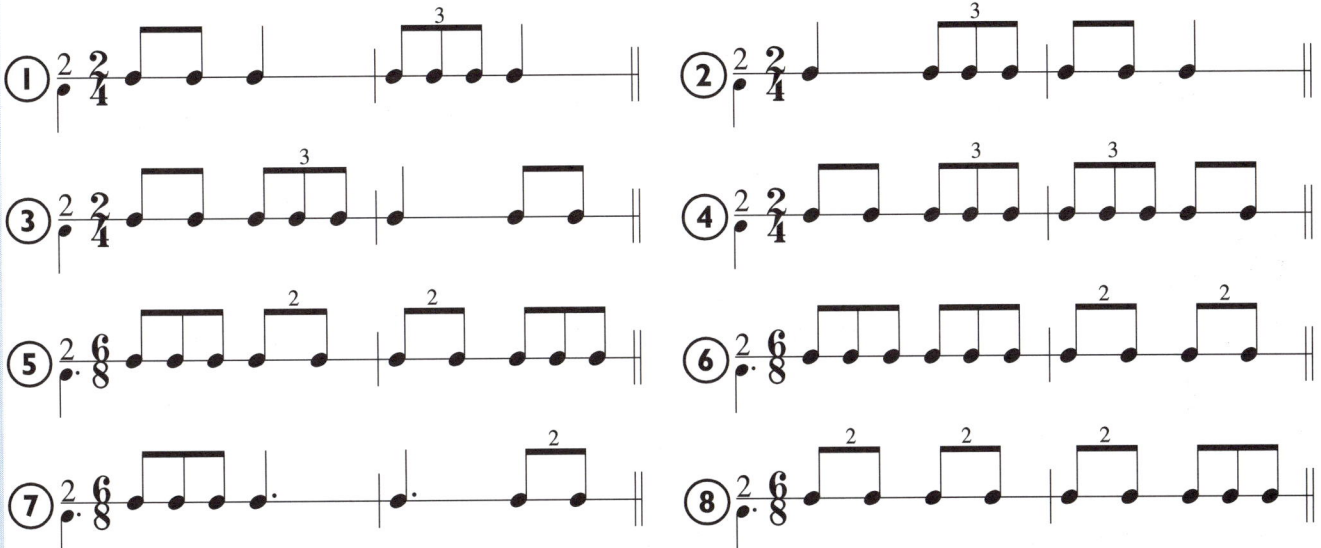

2. Read the following series of patterns by chanting them WITH RHYTHM SYLLABLES and by performing them on your instrument.

   The number (2) tells how many macrobeats there are in a measure.
   The symbol (♪, ♪·) indicates the kind of note that is a macrobeat.

Be expressive when performing with your voice and with your instrument!

MONKEY SONG

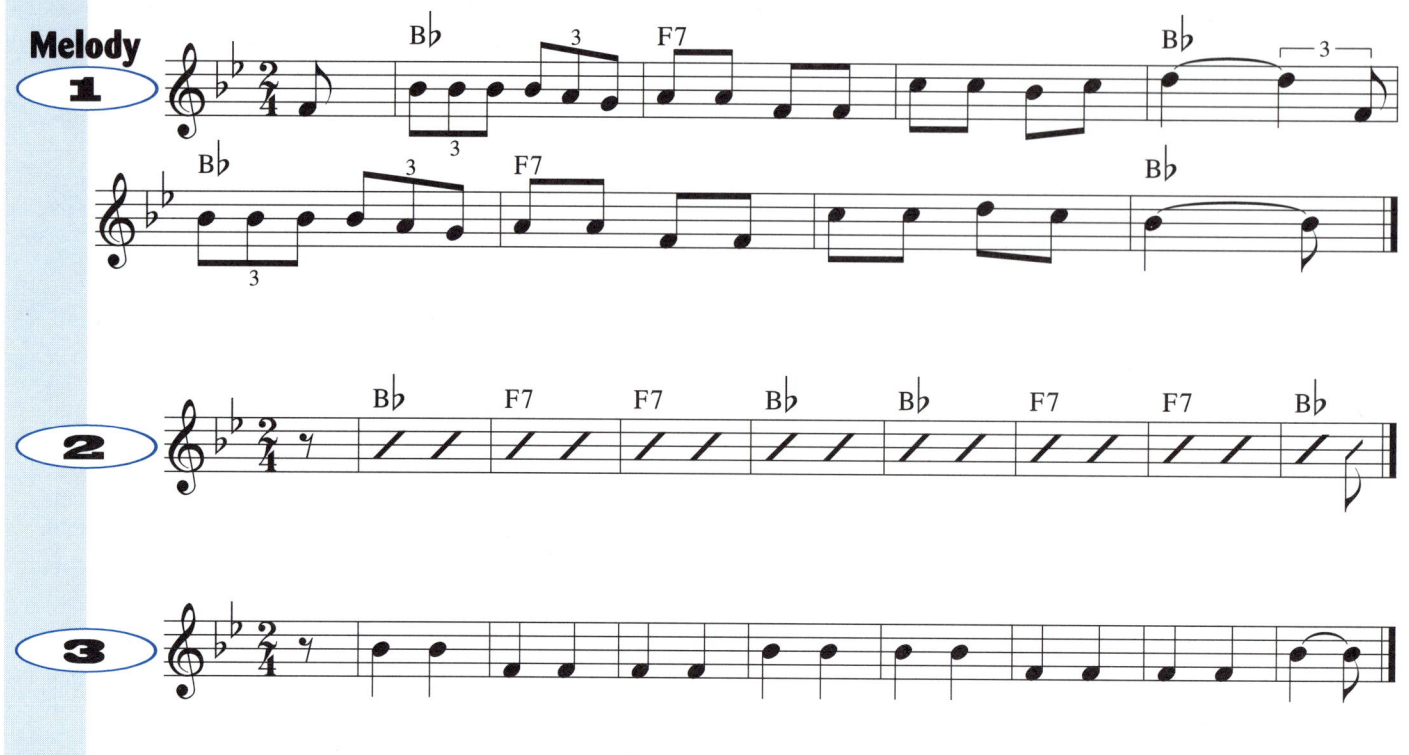

THE BANKS OF NEWFOUNDLAND

TONAL SIGHT READING

1. Sight read the following tonal patterns by singing them WITH A NEUTRAL SYLLABLE and by performing them on your instrument. Some of the patterns are familiar and some are unfamiliar. The arrow points to DO.

RHYTHM SIGHT READING

1. Sight read the following rhythm patterns by chanting them WITH A NEUTRAL SYLLABLE and by performing them on your instrument. Some of the patterns are familiar and some are unfamiliar.

The numbers (2, 1, 3) tell how many macrobeats there are in a measure.
The symbols (♩ or ♩.) indicate the kind of note that is a macrobeat.

MELODIC SIGHT READING

1. Audiate one of the following melodies. If necessary, SING INDIVIDUAL TONAL PATTERNS WITH TONAL SYLLABLES, and CHANT INDIVIDUAL RHYTHM PATTERNS WITH RHYTHM SYLLABLES. DO NOT SING THE ENTIRE MELODY WITH TONAL SYLLABLES. YOU MAY CHANT THE ENTIRE MELODIC RHYTHM USING RHYTHM SYLLABLES.

2. Audiate that melody while performing it silently on your instrument.
3. Perform that melody on your instrument.

MUSIC THEORY

I. Music Symbols

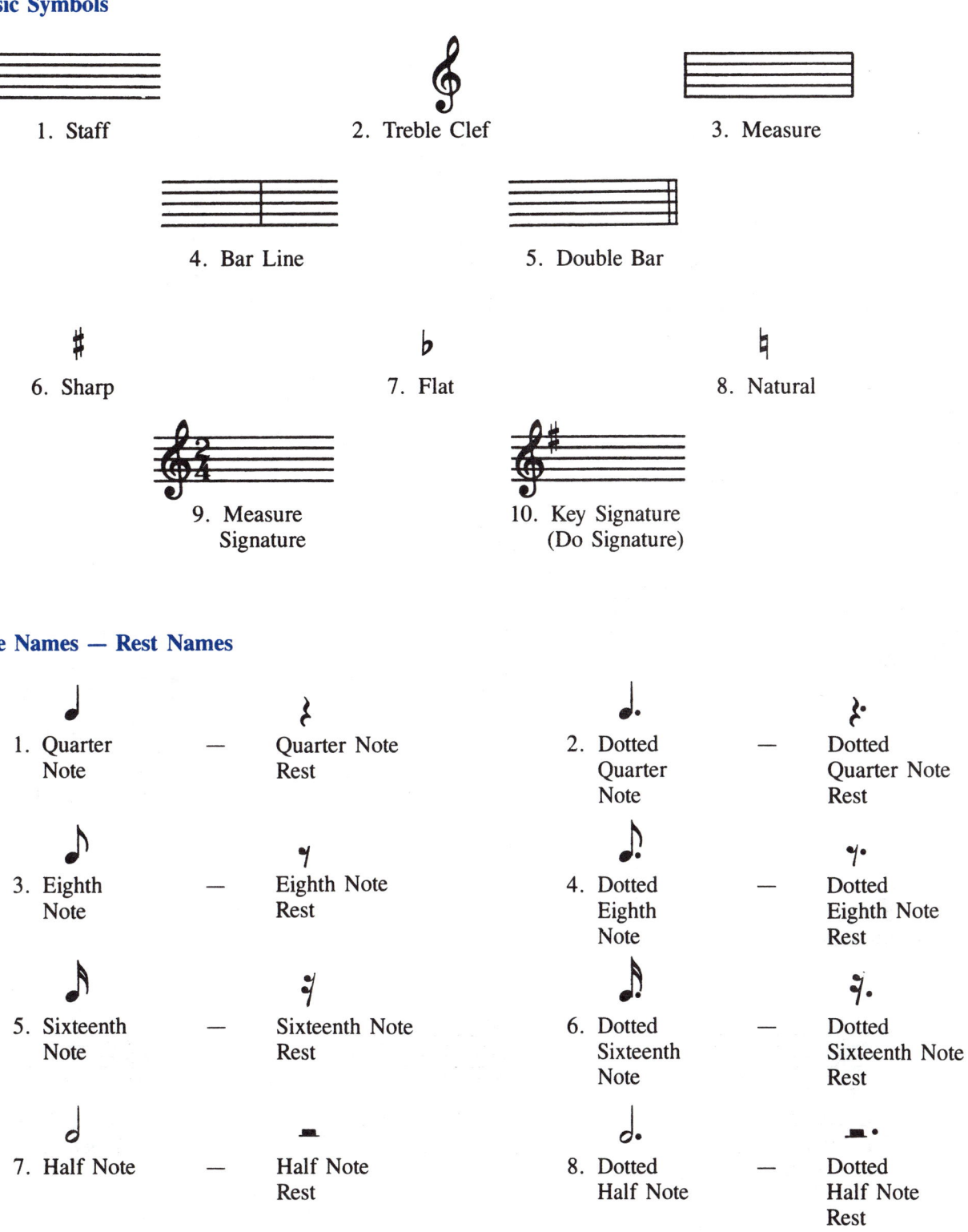

1. Staff   2. Treble Clef   3. Measure

4. Bar Line   5. Double Bar

6. Sharp   7. Flat   8. Natural

9. Measure Signature   10. Key Signature (Do Signature)

II. Note Names — Rest Names

1. Quarter Note — Quarter Note Rest   2. Dotted Quarter Note — Dotted Quarter Note Rest

3. Eighth Note — Eighth Note Rest   4. Dotted Eighth Note — Dotted Eighth Note Rest

5. Sixteenth Note — Sixteenth Note Rest   6. Dotted Sixteenth Note — Dotted Sixteenth Note Rest

7. Half Note — Half Note Rest   8. Dotted Half Note — Dotted Half Note Rest

9. Whole Note — Whole Note Rest   10. Dotted Whole Note — Dotted Whole Note Rest

III. Measure Signatures

$\frac{2}{4}$

1. Two-four

$\frac{4}{4}$

2. Four-four

¢

3. alla breve (cut time)

$\frac{6}{8}$

4. Six-eight

$\frac{3}{8}$

5. Three-eight

$\frac{3}{4}$

6. Three-four

IV. Note Letter Names

Lines

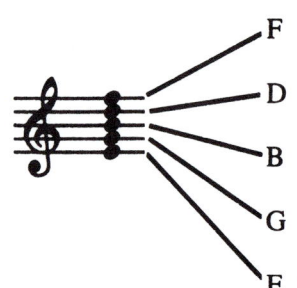

F
D
B
G
E

Spaces

E
C
A
F

Ledger Lines

G   A   B   C

D   C   B   A

V. Key Signatures (DO Signatures)

C Major, A Minor,
D Dorian, etc.
(C is DO)

G Major, E Minor,
A Dorian, etc.
(G is DO)

D Major, B Minor,
E Dorian, etc.
(D is DO)

F Major, D Minor,
G Dorian, etc.
(F is DO)

Bb Major, G Minor,
C Dorian, etc.
(Bb is DO)

Eb Major, C Minor,
F Dorian, etc.
(Eb is DO)